Christmas '18

Dear Jacob,

Your Mom wanted me to write something.
I am. :)

Merry Christmas! I'm very proud of you +
love you very much. I pray this coming

ENDURING
FAITH GAINS
APPROVAL

year is a great me for you. Take time to enjoy
your family + your life. Live a life of enduring
faith. This is it. I've tried to figure a lot of
stuff out and have come to the conclusion
that not much matters but this. Whatever you do
or don't do, always believe that what God says is
true!
        I love you!
                    Dad.

ENDURING
FAITH GAINS
APPROVAL

Focusing on Faith Instead
of the Manifestation

JERRY GRIESER

XULON PRESS

Xulon Press
2301 Lucien Way #415
Maitland, FL 32751
407.339.4217
www.xulonpress.com

Unless otherwise indicated, Scripture quotations taken from the
New American Standard Bible (NASB). Copyright © 1960, 1962,
1963, 1968, 1971, 1972, 1973, 1975, 1977, 1995 by The Lockman
Foundation. Used by permission. All rights reserved.

Printed in the United States of America.

ISBN-13: 978-1-54564-664-9

CONTENTS

INTRODUCTION

**"It is good to have an end to journey toward
but it is the journey that matters in the end."**
Ursula K. LeGuin

This sentiment encompasses the subject of *Enduring Faith
Gains Approval*. In this work, our focus will be on the faith
walk itself rather than focusing on the manifestations of faith. Peter,
in his first letter (1:7), informed us that our faith is more precious
than gold. Faith is the only thing. Faith supersedes the very things
it manifests. *Enduring Faith Gains Approval* is for those who have
a passion for faith, not a quick fix.

We explore the faith battles of the veterans named in Faith's
Hall of Fame, whose primary mode of operation was "what can
I give." Until we exchange our "what can I get" attitude of self-in-
terest toward faith, for "what can I give with faith," we will not be
ready to do battle alongside the veterans, nor share in their success. We will not be ready for the manifestations of God. Why?
Because the very things that defeat us in the negative will destroy
us in the positive.

Living by our flesh or by our senses in victory and success can
be just as disastrous as doing so in failure. If we get offended by

the negative or by failure, that same "sense realm trait" will trip us up in victory. It will show itself in different forms but it comes from the same root. Pride and offense share the same root. Ego and malice flow from the same stream.

We all desire to see the manifestation of God, and God desires to display it. But are we ready for it? Are we living apart from self on the negative side, so we may humbly enjoy the positive when it arrives? Self is ugly when exposed by Satan's works. But self is monstrous when it arises from the manifestations of God. Now I am not saying this is the reason we may not be seeing the manifestations. In fact, *Enduring Faith Gains Approval* specifically does not address the reasons why we do not see instantaneous manifestations, but rather addresses what we are to do in the mean time. It explains what we are to do in the process of, until and after, the manifestation. We will see that some of these veterans' *enduring faith* was put to the test after the manifestation came.

Whether in the victory of seeing faith's manifestation, or the feelings of defeat encountered in its absence, *Enduring Faith Gains Approval* is beneficial and inspirational because of faith's objective in this work. I believe this message is more than a "crossroad" of the faith walk. I believe it to actually be a "border crossing" taking us into another country.

Enduring Faith Gains Approval takes us through a mini Old Testament Survey as we explore how enduring faith was manifested in the lives of the veterans in Faith's Hall of Fame in Hebrews 11. I pray that as you view their experiences in the following exhibits you would be able to transfer what is seen and heard to the "adventure" you are experiencing with God.

Part 1

THE MASTER ARCHITECT AND FAITH'S HALL OF FAME

Chapter 1

FAITH'S HALL OF FAMERS GAINED APPROVAL THROUGH THEIR FAITH

Faith, faith teaching, standing in faith, walking by faith......
depending on your doctrinal persuasion these words can bring
eager expectation, a shudder, or a cynical chuckle. So-called "faith
preachers" are accused of preaching a "name it and claim it, blab
it and grab it" gospel which is regarded by many as too "faith-filled"
and unrealistic. Some Christians choose to avoid the issue while
others are eager to debate. Faith *is* the core of our relationship
with Jesus. The writer of Hebrews declared, *"Without faith it is
impossible to please God"* (Hebrews 11:6).

Where is the balance of walking by faith, believing God for what
He says is reality and the emphasis that invariably gets placed on
the manifestations that faith is intended to produce? Is it possible
that *enduring* faith is the end, in and of itself, and not simply the
means by which we appropriate the blessings of God, whether
they are material possessions or success in life and ministry?

I believe the Bible reveals to us in all its stories that we may
be placing too much emphasis on the wrong element, the outcome. This is easy to do since we live in an outcome based society.

Everything we are encouraged to embrace or purchase is for the purpose of efficiency. Embrace "X" philosophy and you will be guaranteed outcome "Y." Purchase item "A" and the outcome will surely be a magnificent "B". In our society we have been trained, from little on up, to emphasize the destination over the journey. The Bible stories and the story of the Bible emphasize the journey over the destination. It is these stories we want to explore in "Enduring Faith Gains Approval."

Faith's Hall of Famers Gained Approval through Their Faith

The stories of stars and athletes are told in the Halls of Fame for basketball, football, rock and roll, and more. Their journey of struggling to reach their goals is chronicled in pictures and artifacts in booths devoted to their achievement. People in awe of these hall-of-famers, and those who dream of emulating their achievements, visit the halls, which are often designed by very significant architects.

The *Master Architect* has designed Faith's Hall of Fame to display for us the stories of the journeys of men and women who walked a life of enduring faith. A brief description of this hall of fame and their lives are chronicled in Hebrews 11. In this work we will be traveling through Faith's Hall of Fame viewing the exhibits and booths that re-enact the adventures of heroes of faith.

These men and women of enduring faith, those who saw manifestations and those who did not, gained approval through their faith (Heb. 11:39). They gained approval through their faith regardless of whether they escaped the edge of the sword or were put to death by it. None of them received what was promised. Obviously, the emphasis in this hall of fame was not on achieving the manifestation, but on the walk of enduring faith.

Therefore, in this teaching, faith will always be adjectivised with the word "enduring." The subject of this teaching is not faith, but rather "enduring faith". To begin this teaching we are going to look at a portion of the letter to the Hebrews with a view to "endurance". But first I want to give you a picture of where we are heading by stating the "summation" of *Enduring Faith Gains Approval*.

The summation is derived from the primary text of the teaching, Hebrews 10:32-12:11 (NASB). In this text we will find nine *"ences"* that heavily influence our journey of enduring faith. It will do us very well to pay close attention to these *"ences"* as the Holy Spirit teaches us how to walk in enduring faith. These nine *"ences"* are listed in the summation in the order that they are revealed in the text:

The Summation of Enduring Faith Gains Approval

Your confid*ence* pushes you to endur*ance*, giving you the assur*ance* that your rever*ence* to His Word will give you an inherit*ance* that will flow to your descend*ants*, which you view from a dist*ance*, in spite of your experi*ence*! So lay aside every encumbr*ance* to your confid*ence*!

This is where we are going. We want to get to a place where we lay aside every encumbrance to our confidence. And there are encumbrances. But they are nothing new, for God shows us examples of men and women of old who laid encumbrances aside to walk in enduring faith.

Paying Attention to the *"ENCES"*

Our enduring faith journey begins by exploring this passage in Hebrews with a view to endurance:

"But remember the former days, when, after being enlightened, you endured a great conflict of sufferings, partly by being made a public spectacle through reproaches and tribulations, and partly by becoming sharers with those who were so treated. For you showed sympathy to the prisoners, and accepted joyfully the sei-zure of your property, knowing that you have for yourselves a better possession and an abiding one. Therefore do not throw away your <u>confidence</u> (1st "ence"), *which has a great reward"* (Hebrews 10:32-35).

Here we have our first *"ence"*. Paying attention to the *"ences"* we see that our first *"ence"* is "confidence". Our instruction here is to not throw confidence away because it has a great reward. We will discover what that reward is as we evaluate the confidence of those who have gone before us.

Verse 36 of Hebrews 10 states, *"For you have need of <u>endur-ance</u>* (2nd "ence"), *so that when you have done the will of God, you may receive what was promised."* Here is the second *"ence"*. Endurance is a significant part of our title, *Enduring Faith Gains Approval*. We will find that all the rest of the *"ences"* hinge on these first two. God says that we need endurance so that when we have done His will we may receive what was promised.

What is His will? Hebrews 10:35 tells us His will, *"Do not throw away your confidence."* Verse 38 in Hebrews 10 again tells us His will, *"My righteous one shall live by faith."* His will is that you do not throw away your confidence, but continue to endure in walking and living by faith. The context of this scripture teaches that God's righteous ones live by faith. They survive and even thrive in this life against the onslaught of the enemy by faith. Enduring faith.

Keeping your *confidence* will push you to *endurance*, giving you the *assurance* that your *reverence* to His Word will give you an *inheritance* that will flow to your *descendants*, which you view from a *distance*, in spite of your *experience*.

So why lay aside every *encumbrance* to your *confidence*? The answer is in Hebrews 10:37, *"For yet in a very little while, He who is coming will come, and will not delay."* It is only for a little while. He is coming. But in the meantime, God tells us *"My righteous one shall live by faith; and if he shrinks back, my soul has no pleasure in him"* (Hebrews 10:38). To what would he shrink back? He would shrink back to living by the senses, by feelings, and by what he *sees* instead of the promises. That is a walk toward destruction, a walk separate from God. It is a walk God does not derive the pleasure of intimacy He desires from walking with you!

This is the message of *Enduring Faith Gains Approval;* continuing to walk hand in hand with God, believing what He said, regardless of what you see with your eyes or experience in your life. Hebrews 10:39 is a prophetic statement concerning us, God's children, *"But we are not of those who shrink back to destruction, but of those who have faith to the preserving of the soul."* We are those who have faith, enduring faith, to the preserving of our thinking, to continue to think like God thinks, regardless of what we see. Enduring faith will allow you to preserve your thinking. You will be able to keep your thoughts "higher than man's thoughts". You will be able to keep your ways "higher than man's ways" in the midst of all evidence to the contrary.

Enduring faith is an attitude that lives by the spiritual axiom, "What God says is true regardless of my circumstances and experiences. God's words are true regardless of what I see, what I hear, or what I feel." This is the kind of faith that will receive what was promised.

God explains this kind of faith in Hebrews 11:1 (Amp), where we find our third *"ence"*–assurance. *"Now faith is the assurance (the confirmation, the title deed) of the things [we] hope for, being the proof of things [we] do not see and the conviction of their reality [faith perceiving as real fact what is not revealed to the senses]."* What you see with your eyes and what you feel in your body is not the evidence or proof of the promises. Faith is; the type of faith that doesn't quit; faith that isn't thrown away when obstacles are tossed in the path. Enduring faith that gives you the *assurance* that your *reverence* to His Word will give you an *inheritance* that will flow to your *descendants*, which you view from a *distance*, in spite of your *experience*. So lay aside every *encumbrance* to your *confidence*. God is talking to us today.

In Hebrews 11:2 God says by this kind of faith men of old gained approval. *Enduring faith gains approval.* The foundation of this kind of faith is built on the Word of God. The implication is that the very beginning of this faith is premised on understanding that all of creation was prepared by that Word, *"By faith we understand that the worlds were prepared by the word of God, so that what is seen was not made out of things which are visible"* (Hebrews 11:3). This example, given by God, shows us that the evidence of the promises is not based on what is seen. How many times do we give up on the promises, throw away our confidence (our 1st

8

and foundational *"ence"*), just because we didn't or don't "see" the evidence with our eyes. God is telling us something here.

This kind of faith was lived by some now famous "enduring faith walkers". Keep in mind that they were not famous during their "walk". Their walk is what made them famous. With 20/20 hindsight, it may look like they just put it on cruise control and went rolling down the highway of life. However, many of them had no idea where God was taking them. For most it was a hard walk, and for some, it appears to end in failure. But God shows us a different picture than one seen with human eyes.

Chapter 2

ENDURING FAITH WALKERS ABEL, ENOCH, AND NOAH

Enduring Faith Walker, Abel

G od takes us all the way back to the first generation for His first example, Abel.

This first example is one that appears to end in failure when Cain murders his brother Abel. Yet God calls it a success. *"By faith Abel offered to God a better sacrifice than Cain, through which he obtained the testimony that he was righteous, God testifying about his gifts, and through faith, though he is dead, he still speaks"* (Hebrews 11:4). Abel lived by faith and this faith obtained for him the testimony that he was righteous.

We think that this faith walking life of Abel's ended in tragedy, but God says that through that life, that faith walking life, Abel still speaks, even though he is dead. Abel died a premature death but his faith still speaks. His faith still lives. This is key. If we can simply understand that this truth *is* just as applicable today, it would change the way we talk in the midst of negative circumstances.

Will our faith still speak after we have left this earth, regardless of the events leading up to our departure? Will our words depict a "Let God be true and every man a liar" attitude at the time of our departure? Or will the words from our mouth give credence to the world's view, the medical report, or religion's sight inspired clichés? I pray that our faith would speak for as many generations as Abel's has, and pray we would determine to set our faces like flint regardless of the circumstances and evidence to the contrary, declaring we will "let God be true and every man a liar" (Romans 3:4).

Enduring Faith Walker, Enoch

Our next example of an enduring faith walker is Enoch, who *"walked with God and was not."* This is God's desire; that we would walk with Him until we are not, until the "I" is out of "us" and the "me" is out of "we". *"By faith Enoch was taken up so that he should not see death; and he was not found because God took him up; for he obtained the witness that before his being taken up he was pleasing to God"* (Hebrews 11:5). Genesis 5 tells us that Enoch walked with God for 300 years. How? It was by faith. 300 years. That is enduring faith.

After telling us that walking by faith brings Him pleasure, God shows us numerous examples of men and women who brought Him pleasure by doing exactly that. There is no particular pattern of occupation, ministry, life, or outcome that is followed except a pattern of enduring faith in God and His promises regardless of what was seen. Enoch was pleasing to God because of his faith. His life ended, or actually continued, in victory, with Enoch never having to taste physical death to this day.

The first two examples given show the opposite ends of the spectrum; a "faith walking" life prematurely cut short by murder, and one that has not yet ended in death. What a contrast. Both lives live on in these men's "living faith" that still speaks. And now, in Hebrews 11:6, God reiterates that it is faith and only faith by which men must seek Him, *"And without faith it is impossible to please Him, for he who comes to God must believe that He is, and that He is a rewarder of those who seek Him."* There is no other way to please Him. Any other way puts the credit to man, giving man the pleasure, not God. God is the rewarder. Man cannot reward himself for his own efforts. God says, "I will reward those who walk with me in a faith walking life believing that I am who I say I am and that I will do what I said I will do."

Enduring Faith Walker, Noah

Noah is a faith walking man who for years stood in faith believing that what God spoke to him, *would* happen even though there was no evidence that it would ever happen or even that it could. *"By faith Noah, being warned by God about things not yet seen, in reverence prepared an ark for the salvation of his house-hold, by which he condemned the world, and became an heir of the righteousness which is according to faith"* (Hebrews 11:7). It is in this verse that we find our fourth *"ence"*–reverence. Your *reverence* to His Word will give you an *inheritance* that will flow to your *descendants*, which you view from a *distance*, in spite of your *experience*. So lay aside every *encumbrance* to your *confidence*.

Noah was warned about things "not yet seen." And yet "in reverence," that is, in exalting the Word of God above his senses, he devoted his life and his energy to preparing the ark. While we may not be able to determine the exact number of years Noah stood in faith building the ark, the magnitude of the project indicates that it could have been decades. Decades spent gathering the materials, preparing them, and assembling them into the largest floating vessel known to man at that time. The Word of God was in total contradiction to all physical evidences and science available to Noah. Think about the faith required not only to prepare for this event, but also to believe that following such an event, survival would even be possible.

Noah was a real man with real thoughts that bombarded him about the present and the future. "Did God really tell me to do this? Am I just wasting my time? What happens on the other side of this deal? How is this going to affect my family?" These questions bombard any man or woman who has had God ask them to do something out of the ordinary. But Noah was faithful, and by *enduring faith,* built the ark for the salvation of his household and thereby became an heir of the righteousness, which is according to faith. Enduring faith gains approval.

What is enduring faith? The definition of "endure" is to harden the heart, to harden, hold out, last, to hold up under (pain, fatigue, etc.), to continue in existence; last; remain." Under "enduring" we find, "lasting; permanent; durable," and endurance is defined as "the ability to last, continue or remain, ability to stand pain, distress, fatigue; fortitude".

It is clear from these definitions that to walk in enduring faith is to harden one's heart to anything that is in opposition to the things for which one believes, and to continue in that position regardless of the ensuing feelings derived from that opposition. This is not a principle we have been trained to live by. We live in a "timetable" society. Our culture has us mapping out our lives – 13 years of school, 4 years of college, begin career at x amount of salary, expect annual increases of x percent, accumulate wealth, retire at age x. In this society we expect things to happen the *way* we plan for them to happen and *when* we plan for them to happen. Then we get disturbed when they don't. This mindset is prevalent in the children of the Kingdom as well.

Your Confid*ence* Pushes You to Endur*ance*

Even in the midst of this "timetable" planning, most believers truly desire to be *Acts 20:32* people. *"And now I commend you to God and to the word of His grace, which is able to build you up and to give you the inheritance among all those who are sancti-fied."* They truly believe that the Word of His grace will build them up and give them the inheritance. So what is the problem? Why the frustration? What is missing? Hebrews 6:12 is.

In Hebrews 6:12 God encourages us, *"that you may not be sluggish, but imitators of those who through faith and patience inherit the promises."* Clearly, God's Word and faith in His Word is designed to build us up and give us *the* inheritance, God's prom-ises to us. From time to time, many of us, as God's children, exhibit faith in God's word and faith in His promises, but what we lack is the endurance factor. The writer of Hebrews stated that it was through faith *and patience* that they inherited the promises. So what is it we are missing? Patience! And what is it that keeps patience out of our reach? Let's go back once again to our summation.

"Your confid*ence* pushes you to endur*ance*, giving you the assur*ance* that your rever*ence* to His Word will give you an inherit*ance* that will flow to your descend*ants*, which you view from a dist*ance*, in spite of your experi*ence*! So lay aside every encumbr*ance* to your confid*ence*!"

It is confidence that pushes us to endure. The element that keeps endurance out of reach is a lack of confidence. Seeing that confidence is one of our foundational *"ences"* and one that God told us not to throw away, let's explore its definition. Webster's defines the root word, confide, in this way: "to trust in someone—to entrust a duty, object or person to someone." Entrust means to assign the care of, turn over for safekeeping. Isn't that exactly what we are to do? We are to entrust the duties of caring for us to the Someone who said He would take care of us. God's Word implores us to entrust our objects, even our very persons to the Someone who spoke us into being. We are "a spoken Word", a spoken Word of God, and if this is what "confide" means, then we need to confide in the Someone who spoke that Word. We need to confide in Jesus. Doing so is what produces this confidence we need to push us to endurance. Confidence is defined in this way, "firm belief; trust; reliance – the fact of being or feeling certain; assurance – object of trust."

So we see that "confiding" in Jesus is what produces this "confidence" that pushes you to endur*ance*, giving you the assur*ance* that your rever*ence* to His Word will give you an inherit*ance*, that will flow to your descend*ants*, which you view from a dist*ance*, in spite of your experi*ence*. It all hinges on "confidence". This "confiding" is what Noah must have lived, in order to produce the confidence needed to "stand" for years, walking "confidently" in

15

enduring faith, exalting God's Word about things "not yet seen" above his senses. Noah had a vision. He had a ministry. He had a work to do for God. Yet Noah's vision and his ministry were held in contempt by the viewpoint of the majority. His viewpoint was an exceedingly minority viewpoint. For many, many years His ministry was the minority view, until he got on the ark. When he boarded the ark he suddenly held the majority view. But he had to endure, by faith, the laborious years of minority status before he became one of majority status.

Validation by Valuation

How did Noah do it? He did it with "validation by valuation". He did it by employing the "act of determining the value". Validation simply means "to establish as truth or fact". Valuation is "the act of determining the value". How did Noah endure decades of minority status? He did it by establishing as truth, what God had told him. He did this through the act of determining that God's Word was of greater, much greater, value than the opinion of man.

Noah received his validation by his valuation of God's Word. The two are inextricably linked, for validation by any other means will surely pass away (Matthew 24:35). How long though, did Noah have to hold on to his validation by valuation? How long did he have to esteem the Word of God over the word of man, over his senses? It had to have been decades. Again, the definition of endure: "ability to last, continue, or remain; lasting; permanent, durable." Noah exemplified this definition in devoting his life to building God's ark. This concept of endurance is difficult because of that "timetable" society we live in.

We want to rise above the "timetable" factor and imitate those who through faith *and patience* inherit the promises. That is what we will do in *Enduring Faith Gains Approval*. We will look at men and women who, "with patience", walked in faith, believing God *in spite* of, *in defiance* of, and *regardless* of what they saw or perceived! Right now, looking at Noah, we ask how he could endure for decades, standing alone believing God. The answer is in our summation; his confidence pushed him to endurance.

All the people God gives as examples of enduring faith understood patience. They all placed their hope in God. That hope, that "confiding" in God, activated or motivated them to enduring faith. Each of them acted on their faith. All of them had corresponding action to their words. They acted like they believed what God said.

In essence, they turned the thermostat up and took off their coats because they knew the heat was coming. (See *Hope, Faith, & Patience* illustration on page 19). Then they waited patiently, while actively believing for the manifestation of God's promise against all odds. They were sure of it, as sure as the husband who, after turning on the furnace, responds to his wife's complaint "that it's still cold," with "Just wait. I turned it on." That is a statement of faith! If he was not sure, he wouldn't respond that way. His actions reflect his belief. If he gets up and goes to get the toolbox in response to her comment, it indicates that he does not believe it is working. How many of us say, "I believe God. I believe it is working," but have our toolbox out tearing apart the furnace? Noah believed it was working, and he had the "capacity of calm endurance" that lasted for decades, taking his viewpoint from minority status to extreme majority. How did he do it? He had confidence in the unseen realm and saw the spiritual realm as a greater "reality" than the physical or seen realm.

Words and Actions in the Duration Define Enduring Faith

We have need of patience. We have need of enduring faith. So God shows us a variety of examples of men and women who exhibited "enduring faith" with a myriad of results, but who always gained approval by their enduring faith. By doing it in this manner He eliminates any measuring stick or formula for determining by the outcome whether or not enduring faith was exhibited. Instead, it is always the words and actions of each individual in the duration to the outcome that defines "enduring faith". The outcome does not define enduring faith. This is key if you want your faith, like Abel's, to "still speak, though you are dead" (Hebrews 11:4).

HOPE, FAITH AND PATIENCE

YOU CAN'T HAVE ONE WITHOUT THE OTHER - ROM 8 : 24-25

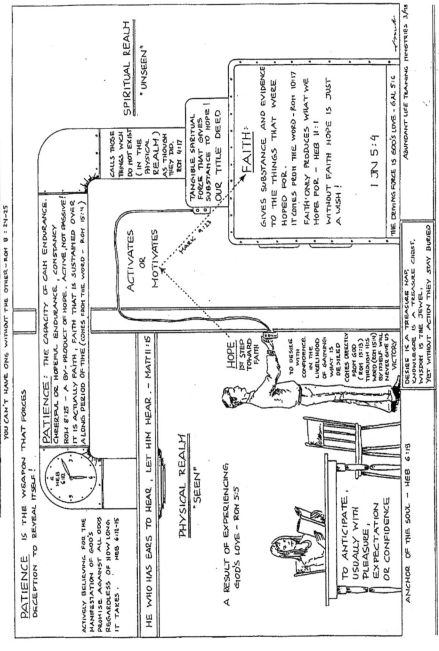

SPIRITUAL REALM "UNSEEN"

CALLS THOSE THINGS WHICH DO NOT EXIST (IN THE PHYSICAL REALM) AS THOUGH THEY DID. ROM 4:17

TANGIBLE SPIRITUAL FORCE THAT GIVES SUBSTANCE TO HOPE! OUR TITLE DEED

FAITH:

GIVES SUBSTANCE AND EVIDENCE TO THE THINGS THAT WERE HOPED FOR.

IT COMES FROM THE WORD - ROM 10:17

FAITH ONLY PRODUCES WHAT WE HOPE FOR - HEB 11:1

WITHOUT FAITH HOPE IS JUST A WISH!

1 JN 5:4

THE DRIVING FORCE IS GOD'S LOVE - GAL 5:6

ABUNDANT LIFE TRAINING MINISTRIES 3/08

ACTIVATES OR MOTIVATES

MARK 9:23

PATIENCE IS THE WEAPON THAT FORCES DECEPTION TO REVEAL ITSELF!

PATIENCE: THE CAPACITY OF CALM ENDURANCE. CHEERFUL OR HOPEFUL ENDURANCE, CONSTANCY
ROM 6:15 - A BY-PRODUCT OF HOPE. ACTIVE, NOT PASSIVE!
IT IS ACTUALLY FAITH, FAITH THAT IS SUSTAINED OVER A LONG PERIOD OF TIME (COMES FROM THE WORD - ROM 15:4)

ACTIVELY BELIEVING FOR THE MANIFESTATION OF GOD'S PROMISE AGAINST ALL ODDS REGARDLESS OF HOW LONG IT TAKES. HEB 6:11-15

HEB 6:12

HE WHO HAS EARS TO HEAR, LET HIM HEAR. - MATT 11:15

PHYSICAL REALM "SEEN"

A RESULT OF EXPERIENCING GOD'S LOVE - ROM 5:5

HOPE
1ST STEP TOWARD FAITH

TO DESIRE WITH CONFIDENCE IN THE LIKELIHOOD OF GAINING WHAT IS DESIRED

COMES DIRECTLY FROM GOD (ROM 15:13) THROUGH HIS WORD (ROM 15:4) BY ITSELF WILL NEVER GIVE US VICTORY

TO ANTICIPATE, USUALLY WITH PLEASURE, EXPECTATION OR CONFIDENCE

DESIRE IS A TREASURE MAP, KNOWLEDGE IS A TREASURE CHEST, WISDOM IS THE JEWEL, YET WITHOUT ACTION THEY STAY BURIED

ANCHOR OF THE SOUL - HEB 6:19

19

Chapter 3

ENDURING FAITH WALKERS
ABRAHAM AND SARAH

Enduring Faith Walker, Abraham

A braham is a man whose faith has resounded, though he is dead, through all generations, and whose faith is woven into almost all religions and written in volumes of literature. It is in Abraham's enduring faith we find our 5th and 6th "ences"–inheritance and descendants.

In Hebrews 11:8-10 we read, *"8 By faith Abraham, when he was called, obeyed by going out to a place which he was to receive for an <u>inheritance</u> (5th "ence"); and he went out, not knowing where he was going. 9 By faith he lived as an alien in the land of promise, as in a foreign land, dwelling in tents with Isaac and Jacob, fellow heirs of the same promise; 10 for he was looking for the city which has foundations, whose architect and builder is God."* Before we expound on these verses jump ahead to verse 12, *"Therefore there was born even of one man, and him as good as dead at that, as many <u>descendants</u> (6th "ence") as the stars of heaven in number, and innumerable as the sand which is by the seashore."*

The word "therefore" clearly indicates that if Abraham had not obeyed "by faith" by going when he was called, and enduring, the many descendents would not have been born. The faith it took to stand as an old man, "and him as good as dead at that," believing that he would someday bear a child, could only come from a lifetime of walking by faith with endurance. The biological clock ticking away against his and Sarah's bodies did not facilitate his faith. Nature, with every passing day, buffeted his faith like the waves against a shore. But because of his enduring faith Abraham could see his inherit*ance* flowing to his descend*ants*, which he viewed from a dist*ance*, in spite of his experi*ence*. His and Sarah's bodies were an encumbr*ance* to his confid*ence*, yet he laid the encumbrance aside and did not consider their bodies.

He had previously exercised and strengthened his faith on a journey to an unknown destination, faith-living in a tent as an alien. How did he do this? God tells us. It is where he focused his eyes. *"for he was looking for the city which has foundations, whose architect and builder is God"* (Hebrews 11:10). Anyone who has been called out by God, and wants to walk in enduring faith, must keep his eyes on the vision, the foundation of that vision, and the architect and builder of that vision. This is what gives you....

....the confid*ence* that pushes you to endur*ance*, giving you the assur*ance* that your rever*ence* to His Word will give you an inherit*ance* that will flow to your descend*ants*, which you view from a dist*ance*, in spite of your experi*ence*! So lay aside every encumbr*ance* to your confid*ence*!

Abraham had a word from God and he followed that word, stood on that word, and believed that word through all of life's difficulties, through all of his own failures, and even when it looked like God was not coming through. Abraham's enduring faith produced the innumerable descendants.

Enduring Faith Walker, Sarah

God gives Abraham's wife as our next example. *"By faith even Sarah herself received ability to conceive, even beyond the proper time of life, since she considered Him faithful who had promised"* (Hebrews 11:11). Her enduring faith allowed her to receive the ability to conceive, even beyond the proper time of life! Why? Because she considered Him faithful! She didn't consider *her* age. She didn't consider *her* faithfulness. She considered *Him* faithful! There is revelation here.

Enduring faith will enable you to receive the ability to conceive. All of us need that ability. Has God shown you things that you feel are 'beyond the proper time of your life'? Has he asked you to do something to which you have responded, "I'm too old". Are there things stirring in your heart that you wish you'd have begun years ago, in your youth? Then this example of enduring faith is for you. It's not about your age. It's not about your ability. Sarah did not *have* the ability to conceive. She *received* the ability to conceive. *It's not about your ability.* It *is* about the faithfulness of Him who has promised and your willingness to bank on that regardless of how stupid it looks or sounds. And it may. Look at our examples.

Enduring Faith is the Point

It looked stupid for Noah to build an ark, for there had never been a forty day and forty night rain. The earth had never experienced anything like a flood. It looked foolish for Abraham to leave a country he knew to go live in tents in a country whose location he didn't even know. It looked stupid for a ninety-year-old woman to believe she could conceive. But believe they did, and with an *enduring faith* that earned them the right to be named as an example of such.

So disregard your age, disregard your inability, and bank on the promise of Him who is faithful. What do you have to lose? You say, "What if it doesn't work? What if it doesn't come to pass?" Don't you see? *That* is not the point. Enduring Faith is the point. *"All these died in faith, without receiving the promises, but having seen them and having welcomed them from a distance* (7ᵗʰ "ence"), *and having confessed that they were strangers and exiles on the earth"* (Hebrews 11:13). All these died in faith. They died believing. Verse 13 is the point.

Regardless of the outcome concerning the physical manifestation of the promise, enduring faith allows you to see and welcome the promises from a distance. *Distance*, our 7ᵗʰ *"ence."* The distance is only as far as the spiritual realm is removed from the physical realm. Knowing this gives you the confid*ence* that pushes you to endur*ance*, giving you the assur*ance* that your rever*ence* to His Word will give you an inherit*ance* that will flow to your descend*ants*, which you view from a dist*ance*, in spite of your experi*ence*! So lay aside every encumbr*ance* to your confid*ence*!"

In this physical realm we are only strangers and exiles, pilgrims passing through to the city, which has foundations. We welcome the promises with our eyes set on that city, that dimension where the promises are not *coming*, but already *are*. We say it didn't work if we don't see it. God says it did work, *if* we say such things that make it clear we are seeking a country of our own. "*For those who say such things make it clear that they are seeking a country of their own*" (Hebrews 11:14).

Our words and actions should make it clear that our sights are set on another country, the spiritual dimension where we see things as they really are – finished, complete, as God says they are. Then those words and actions transcend us from this physical world of the senses to the city of enduring faith in which Abel, Enoch, Noah, Abraham, and Sarah walked, leaving their faith to speak even to this day.

Enduring Faith Gains Approval

If you can say what God says, if you can speak and act on His Word and His promises throughout your journey, then regardless of the outcome, regardless of whether or not you ever see what you are saying you have, your enduring faith will gain approval and will live on, speaking, even though you are dead and gone.

This journey is well described in Psalm 84:5-7 (The Message), "*And how blessed all those in whom you live, whose lives become roads you travel; They wind through lonesome valleys, come upon brooks, discover cool springs and pools brimming with rain! God— traveled, these roads curve up the mountain, and at the last turn— Zion! God in full view!*"

This is what we have to lose if the 'What if it doesn't work?' fear paralyzes us. 'What if it doesn't work?' is only the fear of man. It is only the fear of what others think. How does 'What if it doesn't work' affect you? If it doesn't work, you don't have it either way, so what are you out? You see, 'What if it doesn't work?' doesn't affect you; it effects how you feel others will view you. And that is a snare. Proverbs 29:25 tells us, *"The fear of man brings a snare."* *The Message* says, *"The fear of human opinion disables; trusting in GOD protects you from that."*

The opinions of others can disable you. Others do not have a view of the city you are looking at. They will tell you that you have no foundation, because they cannot see it. But the truth is, what *they* can see is foundationless. It is subject to change (2 Corinthians 4:18). But what *you* can see has an enduring foundation because its architect and builder is God. It is all about where you are looking. The country on which you have set your sights will determine your words and actions. In Heb. 11: 15 God goes on to say that even these faith walking men and women would have had an opportunity to speak and act differently, had they set their sights on the country from which they had come, *"And indeed if they had been thinking of that country from which they went out, they would have had opportunity to return."*

You have been translated out of the kingdom of darkness (this world) into His marvelous light. If you are mindful of, or set your sights on, the country from which you came, you will have opportunity to return to speaking and acting according to that country's way of speaking and acting. You will lose the opportunity for your faith to speak on through the ages.

The faith walking men and women of Hebrews 11 did not lose the opportunity for their faith to speak on. They chose to be mindful of, to speak and act according to a better country, a heavenly one. *"But as it is, they desire a better country, that is, a heavenly one. Therefore God is not ashamed to be called their God; for He has prepared a city for them"* (Hebrews 11:16). Therefore God is not ashamed to be called their God. He says, "Those are my people, they talk just like me. That is my son, he's acting just like I do. Look, there goes my daughter, tenacious and confident, a chip off the old block!" They're living in *His* world, *His* country, *His* city, and they sound like Him, walk like Him, and act like Him. And He says, "I'm their Daddy!"

Who's Your Daddy?

God wants to know that when you are asked, "Who's your daddy?" there'll be no question. He desires enduring faith, faith that declares God is your Father in life and in death, in drought and in flood, in transition and in dwelling, in barrenness and in birth. He wants to know if you really believe it.

In Hebrews 11:7 He shows us His faith man Abraham in another "faith" setting. He says, *"By faith Abraham, when he was tested, offered up Isaac, and he who had received the promises was offering up his only begotten son."* It *was* a test! God wanted to know if *He* was Abraham's Father. After the test was over God said, "Now I know" (Gen. 22:12). It was *by faith* that he passed the test. This is "enduring faith".

This faith in the Father and His promise endured *beyond* the birth of his only begotten son! So confident was Abraham in the promise that he was willing to offer up the provision of that very promise *"it was he to whom it was said, 'in Isaac your descendants shall be called'"* (Heb. 11:18). That is enduring faith. This teaching has been given to us to produce such confidence in the Father and His promise that we are willing to 'offer' up the provision of the promise.

Are you willing to stand in agreement with God, speak His promises, and act like they are true, regardless of whether or not you have possession of the provision? This is enduring faith.

How did Abraham do it? *"He considered that God is able to raise people even from the dead, from which he also received him back as a type"* (Heb. 11:19). He *considered* that God is able. That is what he thought on. He thought on Daddy. He thought on the *'Resurrector'* of the dead. He didn't see Isaac dead. He saw him alive. He spoke of him being alive. At the mountain, with his knife at his side and the fire in his hand, he said to his servants, "<u>We</u> will return," referring to himself and Isaac (Gen. 22:5). He told Isaac, "God will provide for Himself the lamb" (Gen. 22:8). This is how enduring faith speaks, even when faced with evidence to the contrary. Do you speak like Abraham spoke?

Chapter 4

ENDURING FAITH WALKERS ISAAC, JACOB, JOSEPH, AMRAM & JOCHEBED

Enduring Faith Walker, Isaac

We can measure or evaluate whether or not we are walking in enduring faith by the words of our mouth and our corresponding actions. Are you speaking what you see? Are you speaking what you feel? Or are you speaking the things God says are true?

Isaac is the next example God gives us in Hebrews 11:20. *"By faith Isaac blessed Jacob and Esau, even regarding things to come."* Isaac blessed Jacob and Esau. That means he spoke to them concerning their lives. By what did he speak? Was it by what he saw? No, he spoke to them or blessed them by *regarding things to come!* The Amplified says, *"[With eyes of] faith Isaac, looking far into the future, invoked blessings upon Jacob and Esau."*

Enduring Faith Walker, Jacob

Are the words that you speak derived from looking far into the future or looking at what you see now? You say, "How can I see into the future?" The same way every one of God's examples did it, by faith in God's Word. You cannot see into the future without the Word. Jacob, our next enduring faith example, saw into the future and crossed his hands placing the greater blessing on the younger of Joseph's sons, Ephraim over Manasseh (Gen. 48:13-20). God said in Hebrews 11:21 that it was by faith, *"By faith Jacob, as he was dying, blessed each of the sons of Joseph, and worshiped, leaning on the top of his staff."*

Enduring Faith Walker, Joseph

Joseph saw into the future and gave orders to be buried in the land of promise. He "saw" the exodus with eyes of enduring faith, verse 22, *"By faith Joseph, when he was dying, made mention of the exodus of the sons of Israel, and gave orders concerning his bones."* Joseph had his eyes on "another country". He saw the Promised Land and said, "Take my bones there."

Enduring Faith Walkers, Amram and Jochebed

Amram and Jochebed are examples of enduring faith. *"By faith Moses, when he was born, was hidden for three months by his parents, because they saw he was a beautiful child; and they were not afraid of the king's edict"* (Heb. 11:23). With eyes of faith, or as the Amplified Bible reads, *"prompted by faith"*, they hid their son

29

Moses for three months, not fearing the king's edict. Faith allowed them to see into the future and "act" with enduring faith. Amram and Jochebed used eyes of faith to see into the future and acted with enduring faith to save their young son Moses, enabling him to grow up and become God's next example of enduring faith.

Chapter 5

ENDURING FAITH WALKERS MOSES, ISRAEL, AND RAHAB

Enduring Faith Walker, Moses

Hebrews 11:24-25, *"By faith Moses, when he had grown up, refused to be called the son of Pharaoh's daughter, choosing rather to endure ill-treatment with the people of God than to enjoy the passing pleasures of sin."* Moses' faith eyes gave him the courage to relinquish his rights and privileges as Pharaoh's grandson, and his desire to walk in enduring faith allowed him to endure ill-treatment with his own people. Verse 25 starts with the word "Choosing". Moses had a choice. He could have chosen to enjoy the passing pleasures of sin, but he chose the enduring faith walk. How did he do it? Those faith eyes. They were on the greater riches. *"considering the reproach of Christ greater riches than the treasures of Egypt; for he was looking to the reward"* (Heb. 11:26). He saw something greater than the riches he had in the palace. He was looking to the future. He was looking to the reward.

You also have a choice. You can tell what your choice is by listening to your words. Your words depict the location on which your eyes are set. Do your words locate you 'in the present' or 'in the future'? *Enduring faith* will keep you and your words located in the future, even when you are in the wilderness (Heb. 11:27). *"By faith he* (Moses) *left Egypt, not fearing the wrath of the king; for he endured, as seeing Him who is unseen."* With enduring faith he left Egypt with no fear and he *endured*. The Amplified Bible says Moses *"endured steadfastly as one who gazed on Him Who is invisible."*

Gazing on the Invisible

We are talking about the Word here. John 1:1, *"In the beginning was the Word, and the Word was with God, and the Word was God."* If you are to walk this faith walk with enduring steadfastness, if you want to see enduring faith that gains approval, you will need to gaze on the Invisible One who has made Himself visible in His Living Word. Do you see the "truth" disclosed here? How can you gaze on something or someone invisible? You can't. But this Invisible Someone has made Himself visible and has given you eyes of faith to see into this invisible realm if you so choose. Moses made a choice. We can make a choice. Actually it is a series of "enduring faith" choices. For our example man Moses continues to make faith choices against common sense, even against all odds, for the rest of his life.

Paying Attention to the Specifics

In Heb. 11:28-29 God gives us only two of the thousands of faith choices Moses made during his "enduring faith" walk, *"By faith he kept the Passover and the sprinkling of the blood, so that he who destroyed the firstborn would not touch them. By faith they passed through the Red Sea as though they were passing through dry land; and the Egyptians, when they attempted it, were drowned."* These were 'strange', very strange choices. They flew in the face of reason. But we know that these choices required words and actions that were based completely on the Word of God, with absolutely no feelings or opinions allowed to adulterate the situation.

God was always specific. He was specific in Numbers 20:8 when He told Moses to *speak* to the rock in the wilderness of Zin that it may yield its water for the people. In that instance Moses chose not to adhere to the specifics and instead *struck* the rock twice with his rod. In verse 12, God tells Moses and Aaron that because of this they would be prohibited from leading the Israelites into the Promised Land. He said, *"Because you have not believed me* (paid attention to My specifics) *you shall not bring this assembly into the land...."* In Deuteronomy 32:51 God called it *"breaking faith"* with Him. According to Psalm 106:33 Moses spoke rashly in addressing the Israelites in Numbers 20:10. In this one instance Moses failed to pay attention to the specifics and it cost him. But over the course of his faith journey Moses chose God's specifics and ended up with six verses devoted to his *enduring faith* in Faith's Hall of Fame displayed in Hebrews 11.

"What does this have to do with me?" you might ask. God has given us specifics. He said "Rejoice always, again I say rejoice" (Phil. 4:4). Now we can cry out and say, "Lord, I would rather strike the rock than rejoice." but that is not in the specifics. Every time I detour from the specifics, like Moses, it hinders me from walking in the Promised Land. The "always" in rejoice always keeps me walking in the Promised Land.

God has given us specifics. He said, "Let your mind dwell on whatever is true, honorable, right, pure, and lovely" (Phil. 4:8). He said, "Set your mind on the things above, not on the things that are on earth" (Col. 3:2). God said, "Consider it all joy when you encounter various trials" (James 1:2). He said, "Submit therefore to God and resist the devil" (James 4:7). He said, "Put on the Lord Jesus Christ" (Rom. 13:14). God said, "Let no unwholesome word proceed from your mouth, but only such a word as is good for edification" (Eph. 4:29). He said, "Pray without ceasing. In every-thing give thanks" (1Thess. 5:17-18). He said, "Continually offer up a sacrifice of praise" (Heb. 13:15). These are His specifics. His specifics are summed up in this, "Let your mouth line up with My mouth, and let your actions line up with your mouth."

God's ways – His specifics – are more important than His will. Pay attention to His ways and you will be in His will! Are you choosing God's specifics? If so, you are walking in enduring faith and gaining approval. The point in this teaching is not about seeing the manifestation of your faith. The manifestation is secondary to walking in enduring faith. Moses never reached the Promised Land. He lived a lifetime of making enduring faith choices without seeing the manifestation of the promise, yet he has been given one of the largest exhibits in Faith's Hall of Fame.

Keep saying what God said. Keep acting like it is true. Do it week after week, month after month, year after year, regardless of what you see, feel, or experience. It does not matter how much loss you encounter. It does not matter how much failure appears to come your way. If you go to your grave speaking the promises of God and acting like they are true, without ever experiencing them, your faith will live on, speaking to your succeeding generations. Why? Because it is the *enduring faith* walk that gains approval, not the manifestation. It is the process, not the destination.

Of the ten lepers whom Jesus healed, only one gained approval and was told, "Rise and go your way; your faith has made you well" (Luke 17:12-19). It was the one who turned back to give glory to God. All ten received the "manifestation" but only one turned to walk the faith walk, whose faith speaks to this day. This story is not about the ten lepers. This story is about the one leper who was made whole. We don't admire the "faith" of the nine. We don't desire to emulate them. We admire the "faithfulness" of the one.

Enduring Faith is Driving in the Stakes

The faith walk is what lives on and speaks. The manifestation does not. The faith speaks, not the manifestation. People have come and gone in the so-called *faith movement*. Many have grabbed hold of, then let go of the so-called faith message, oftentimes simply based on what they have or have not experienced. *Enduring Faith Gains Approval* is not about the experience. Enduring faith is about driving in the stakes. Enduring faith is about declaring, "I'm in this for life!" Enduring faith walkers desire to have their *faith* speak to succeeding generations regardless of whether or not they see *any* physical manifestations. Enduring faith walkers will gather wood, cut lumber, drive nails, and slap on pitch, month after month, year after year, even if they never see a drop of rain. Like Noah, they turn up the thermostat on their faith and take off their coats. If it takes decades for the heat to come, big deal. It's not about the heat. It's about believing.

Enduring Faith Walkers, Israel

Faith speaks. It is not the fallen walls of Jericho that speak, but as Heb. 11:30 tells us, it is the faith of the people who encircled the walls that speaks to this day, *"By faith the walls of Jericho fell down after they had been encircled for seven days."* For six days straight these people of enduring faith 'foolishly' marched one time around the city in silence. Then on the seventh day after marching around the city seven times they began shouting like a bunch of crazies. But their enduring faith lives on, speaking to us today.

Enduring Faith Walker, Rahab

It is not the walls of Rahab's house that remained standing that speak to us today, but the faith of Rahab that kept those walls up while all the others crumbled. *"By faith Rahab the harlot did not perish along with those who were disobedient, after she had welcomed the spies in peace"* (Heb. 11:31).

Your faith will speak on. Your faith that keeps your walls standing–your walls of hope, joy, gratitude, rejoicing, and endurance–your faith that keeps those walls standing while the walls of those around you crumble, will speak on, echoing through the ages, to generation after generation. And now God says to us in verse 32, "What more do you want?" How many more examples do you need to understand that all I want for you is to bank on My Word, to live your life as though My Word was already a reality in your life?"

Chapter 6

ENDURING FAITH WALKERS GIDEON, BARAK, SAMPSON, JEPHTHAH, DAVID, SAMUEL, THE PROPHETS, AND THE OTHERS

Enduring Faith Walkers: Gideon, Barak, Sampson, Jepthah, David, Samuel, & the Prophets

God says, "I could give you more examples. I could give you details about Gideon, who by faith went from being a wimp to a warrior in an impossible situation. I could tell you about Barak, who by faith, went from being a sissy to a singer of war victories. I could tell you about Sampson, who by faith, went from being a lustful prostitute patron to a blind but powerful pillar pusher who brought judgment on the enemies of My people Israel. If you had the time, I'd share the exploits of Jephthah, who went from being a harlot's son, gang leader, and foolish vow maker to a valiant warrior and a judge over My people."

"I could go on and on about David, My heart man, who by faith, endured years of hardship training to become the leader of the mightiest nation on earth. I could tell you about Samuel, who by faith, lived through the arid years of Saul's reign, watching a spirit of evil arise in the leader whom he had anointed. By faith he *waited* for the day that the man "after My own heart" would take the throne. I could describe the faith walk of all My prophets, from Isaiah to Malachi, but how much time do you have? Let's suffice it to say," God says in Hebrews 11:33-35, that "all these men and women, by faith conquered kingdoms, by faith performed acts of righteousness, by faith obtained promises, by faith shut the mouths of lions, by faith quenched the power of fire, by faith escaped the edge of the sword, by faith from weakness were made strong, by faith became mighty in war, by faith put foreign armies to flight, and by faith women even received back their dead by resurrection. And it is their *faith* that lives on and speaks to you today."

God could have gone into great detail describing how these patriarchs of faith stood on His Word, and followed His directions against all the odds and the evidence to the contrary, for *however* long it took, and *wherever* it took them. But for the sake of time He just names them and says that it was their *faith* that produced. It was their faith that delivered. It was their faith by which they endured.

The Enduring Faith of the "Others"

Now God reveals the enduring faith of the *other half* of His faith walkers. *"...and others were tortured, not accepting their release, so that they might obtain a better resurrection;* [36] *and others* expe-rienced *(8*th *"ence") mockings and scourgings, yes, also chains and imprisonment.* [37] *They were stoned, they were sawn in two, they were tempted, they were put to death with the sword; they went about* *in sheepskins, in goatskins, being destitute, afflicted, ill-treated* [38] *(men of whom the world was not worthy), wandering in deserts and mountains and caves and holes in the ground"* (Hebrews 11:35-38).

It is in this passage we find our eighth *"ence"* – experience. Remember, "Your confid*ence* pushes you to endur*ance*, giving you the assur*ance* that your rever*ence* to His Word will give you an inherit*ance* that will flow to your descend*ants*, which you view from a dist*ance*, in spite of your experi*ence*! So lay aside every encumbr*ance* to your confid*ence*!" *In spite of your experience!* These faith walkers experienced torture, not accepting their release. They *didn't* get delivered from the mouths of lions. These faith walkers *didn't* escape the edge of the sword, but were put to death by it in order that they might obtain a better resurrection. These *didn't* conquer kingdoms, but were mocked and scourged. Was it by faith? God says it was. He says it was enduring faith that caused them to choose *"not to accept their release"* but to obey God.

These *didn't* become mighty in war, but were chained and imprisoned. Instead of putting foreign armies to flight, these were stoned and sawn in two. It is said that Isaiah was stuffed into a hollow log and sawn in half. They were tempted; they were put to death with the sword; they went about in sheepskins, in goatskins, being destitute, afflicted, ill-treated. These were men and women of whom this world was not worthy.

They were worthy of another world's approval, though. They chose to wander in deserts and mountains and caves and holes in the ground, rather than to seek the approval of this world. They chose obscurity over worldly notoriety. They chose what was right over what was popular. They chose hardship over unrighteous gain. They chose what God told them to do over what was *easy*.

All of these men and women of enduring faith, those who *saw* manifestations and those who *did not*, gained approval *through their faith*. *"And all these, having gained approval through their faith, did not receive what was promised"* (Hebrews 11:39). They gained approval through their faith regardless of whether they escaped the edge of the sword or were put to death by it. All of these gained approval through their faith, but none of them, *received what was promised.* All of these men and women lived and died in various manifestations of faith, without ever receiving what they truly believed they would receive from God.

What was the promise that they had their sights set on? What was it that they did not receive, even though they got the ark, the promised seed, the Promised Land, the victories, and the conquered kingdoms? What was the promise?

The promise they desired to receive was the promise of the new creation. Their desire to be new creation men and women *surpassed* the desire for success and victory. This is the key to the enduring faith walk. Their desire was to have a new spirit put within them. Their desire was to have God's laws written on their heart. Their desire was to see what you see. Their desire was to have what you have, God's nature and life imparted to them. They wanted more than success and victory. They wanted perfection that only the 'once for all time' sin offering of Jesus Christ could provide. Heb. 11:40 tells us they lived lives of enduring faith without receiving the promise *"because God had provided something better for us, so that apart from us they would not be made perfect."* This was their desire. This is what they longed for. They longed to be made perfect and have no more consciousness of sins (Heb. 10:1-2). They were tired of dragging around the guilt.

Does our desire to walk as new creation men and women sur-
pass our desire for success and victory? If not, then perhaps we
need to adopt their attitude and emulate their *enduring faith* walks,
so that our *enduring faith* may also gain God's approval.

Enduring faith walkers, there ought to be a prophecy in your life
that makes no sense. There ought to be a Word from God in you that
appears impossible. There ought to be a vision in your heart that
only God can fulfill. There ought to be something in you that says,
"God, I'm going to do what you have told me to do no matter how
much it costs, how ridiculous it sounds, or how many go with me."

Understand that you don't need certain people to go with you.
You don't want *some* people to go with you. Some people cannot
go with you. They cannot see what you see. They are not looking
for the city you are looking for. They are unable to wander in the
deserts and the mountains. They are unable to live in caves and
holes in the ground. And they will not understand why you would.
Don't let them hold you back. You are a man or a woman of whom
the world is not worthy. Don't let their words discourage you. Their
priorities are not yours. They are not the builder and the architect
of your life. The carpenter's Son is. Jesus is the architect of your
life! Get His blueprints. Speak His blueprints. Live His blueprints
no matter how ridiculous they look. He knows what you are going
to need. He knows how you need to be built.

How can we adopt the attitudes of these faith walking men and
women? If we are going to emulate them, we must answer this
question, *"what does faith do?"* Take a tour through Faith's Hall of
Fame as we break down and categorize the manifestations or the
demonstration of these witnesses' faith.

The "Manifestations" of Faith
as seen in Hebrews 11

- **Abel: faith's worship**
- **Enoch: faith's walk**
- **Noah: faith's work**
- **Abraham: faith's obedience**
- **Sarah: faith's reckoning**
- **Abraham: faith's test**
- **Isaac: faith's material blessing**
- **Jacob: faith's tribal blessing**
- **Joseph: faith's authority**
- **Amram and Jochebed: faith's recognition**
- **Moses: faith's declaration   faith's fearlessness faith's protection**
- **Israel: faith's preservation faith's miracle**
- **Rahab: faith's deliverance**
- **Gideon: faith's miraculous victory**
- **Barak: faith's triumph**
- **Samson: faith's physical strength**
- **Jephthah: faith's boldness**
- **David: faith's utter reliance**
- **Samuel: faith's integrity**
- **The "Others": faith's consummation**

Adapted from Dake's Annotated Reference Bible – Copyright 1961

Part 2

A TOUR THROUGH FAITH'S HALL OF FAME

Chapter 7

FAITH'S WORSHIP, WALK, WORK, OBEDIENCE, AND RECKONING

Faith's Worship

Beginning our tour in the Hall of Faith we find exhibit #1 labeled, "Faith's Worship". Look, Abel brings to God the fat portions from the firstborn of his flock (Genesis 4:4). God shows favor and respect to Abel for acknowledging his sin and his need of mercy. God declares to Abel that he is justified for acting in faith regarding the coming seed of the woman Who would bruise the serpent's head. Abel apparently acknowledges Christ's blood in type. In this exhibit of *faith's worship* he demonstrates for us a picture of Christ's atonement.

There is Cain, Abel's brother. He has offered the Lord fruit of the ground as his offering. This is not acceptable to the Lord and now Cain is angry. God speaks, *"Why are you angry? And why has your countenance fallen? If you do well, will not your countenance be lifted up? And if you do not do well, sin is crouching at the door, and its desire is for you, but you must master it"* (Genesis 4:6-7). God offers Cain another chance to enter the door of *faith's worship* in a way that will bring Cain favor. Will Cain's anger and pride prevent him from taking advantage of this opportunity? He must master these emotions and follow God's instruction before these emotions consume him.

In the next scene we find Cain and Abel working a field. What is this? Cain obviously is still upset about God favoring Abel's offering. He shouts at Abel. He grabs a rock. Cain swings the rock toward Abel's head. It connects. Blood gushes from the wound. Cain has killed his brother. He was unable to master his emotions and enter through the door of worship.

God approaches Cain in scene 3 of this exhibit. He speaks, *"Where is Abel your brother?"* Cain answers, *"I do not know. Am I my brother's keeper?"* God responds, *"What have you done? The voice of your brother's blood is crying to me from the ground."* This exhibit is about blood, blood that speaks. Abel understood that worship is about the blood. He believed God when He said, *"Without shedding of blood there is no forgiveness"* (Hebrews 9:22). Because Abel believed God about the blood, his own blood speaks even to this day. Abel's blood speaks *faith's worship* to us and points us toward the blood that speaks better than his blood. His blood points us *"to Jesus, the mediator of a new covenant, and to the sprinkled blood, which speaks better than the blood of Abel"* (Hebrews 12:24).

This exhibit is about *speaking blood*. Abel's blood speaks to us about worship and points us to the sprinkled blood of Jesus that speaks much louder. Jesus' blood cries out, "Mercy to you and grace upon grace!" It is the voice of this blood that moves us to fall down and worship. Anyone can enter into faith's worship when they hear the cry of Jesus' blood calling to them. It is His blood that causes us to *"draw near with confidence to the throne of grace, that we may receive mercy and may find grace in the time of need"* (Hebrews 4:16).

Faith's worship is based on the blood. In this exhibit we see that faith is demonstrated in worship, worship as God wants it, in Spirit and in *truth*, recognizing the need of a blood sacrifice. We see Abel kneeling in worship, being justified by faith in Christ's blood, which he acknowledged in type. It cost him his life, but his enduring faith speaks on, through the voice of his blood.

What does faith do? Faith worships! Your *enduring faith* should move you to worship in the same manner. Abel demonstrates for us *faith's worship,* and this is what God says about Abel's example, *"By faith Abel offered to God a better sacrifice than Cain, through which he obtained the testimony that he was righteous, God testifying about his gifts, and through faith, though he is dead, he still speaks"* (Hebrews 11:4). God is not testifying to us of Abel's *gift*, but his *gifts*. In this we see that faith's worship was a regular occurrence for Abel. *Faith's worship* should be a regular occurrence for us as well.

Faith's Walk

At exhibit #2 the sign reads, "Faith's Walk". The first scene of the exhibit is a simple one with only two characters, Enoch and God. It appears that Enoch is simply walking, and walking, and walking, and walking, and walking, and walking with God, hand in hand. The sign says, "Enoch walked with God three hundred years" (Genesis 5:22). 300 years! What does faith do? Faith walks with God, no matter how far, no matter how long.

In the second scene of the exhibit Enoch prophesies. The sign for this scene states, 'Enoch prophesies of the second advent of Jesus Christ and speaks of those who have gone the way of Cain.' He speaks, *"Behold, the Lord came with many thousands of His holy ones, to execute judgment upon all, and to convict all the ungodly of all their ungodly deeds which they have done in an ungodly way, and of all the harsh things which ungodly sinners have spoken against Him"* (Jude 14-15). It doesn't look good for those who refuse to heed the call of "the blood" and enter into the door of faith's worship. Cain must have spoken harshly against God's method and God's way. What does faith do? *Faith walks with God, doing it His way, with a view to the day the Lord will come with many thousands of His holy ones.*

Scene three appears to be more unusual. Enoch rises into the air. He is taken up into heaven with the One he has walked hand in hand with for three hundred years. This scene's sign states: *"Enoch walked with God; and he was not, for God took him"* (Genesis 5:24). The chain of sin and death has been snapped, at least temporarily. This man walked so closely with God that he did not die in his generation, but was translated. The exhibit's epilogue reads, *"By faith Enoch was taken up so that he would not see death; and he was not found because God took him up; for he obtained the witness that before his being taken up he was pleasing to God"* (Hebrews 11:5). It was by faith he was taken up. Enoch's faith has made him the oldest man alive today. He must be approaching 6000 years by now with Elijah pulling a close second. Elijah is the only other human taken to heaven in his natural body.

At the bottom of the epilogue it simply reads, *"...it is appointed for men to die once and after this comes judgment"* (Hebrews

9:27). This must be the Master Architect's subtle way of informing us that only Enoch and Elijah qualify as candidates to return as the two witnesses who will die at the hands of the antichrist (Zech. 4:11-13, Mal. 4:5-6, Rev. 11:3-13). Since it is appointed for men to die once, only Enoch and Elijah still live in their natural bodies and therefore must return to earth where death still reigns in order to die and receive their resurrection bodies. Enoch's enduring faith has temporarily broken the chain of death enabling him to walk with God in his natural body for not only 300 years on earth but close to 6000 years in heaven. This man, in his natural body, has seen the genesis and in his natural body, will see the revelation. What does faith do? Faith walks with God. In a massive way Enoch demonstrates for us *faith's walk.*

Faith's Work

In exhibit #3, "Faith's Work", scene one, we see God grieving in His heart and talking to Himself. *"I will blot out man whom I have created from the face of the land, from man to animals to creeping things and to birds of the sky; for I am sorry that I made them"* (Genesis 6:7). Viewing the great wickedness of man and the evil intent of their hearts, He shakes his head, frustrated about what He must do. He spots Noah, a standout among the evil. A look of favor spreads across God's face. He makes His way over to Noah saying, "I have a plan!" *"Make for yourself an ark of gopher wood; you shall make the ark with rooms, and shall cover it inside and out with pitch"* (Genesis 6:14). God gives Noah all the details for this project that will save him and his family from the coming destruction, a massive worldwide flood that will destroy all flesh.

Out of reverence to God's word regarding things not yet seen, Noah, moved by faith, put action behind his words" (Hebrews 11:7). In scene two of this exhibit, Noah cuts a tie-beam. His sons make pins and trestles, and their women prepare vats of pitch to coat the inside and outside of the ark. This is a massive project. There are organized piles of shiplap lumber, assembled trusses, and wooden pins lying all around the assembly site. This work team has built assembly scaffolding around the skeleton of the ark and six rigging cranes on the structure itself. Noah has several blueprint tables set up and pores over the prints at the stern. The organization and logistics of Noah's materials appear to be immaculate and efficient. Noah demonstrates *faith's work* for us.

What does faith do? *Faith works.* Faith doesn't wait for a handout from God, but takes the blueprints He gives and goes to work. Like Enoch, *"Noah walked with God"* (Genesis 6:9). However, enduring faith does more than just walk with God, it works. Faith is 'belief in action'. Faith understands that God is the designer and the architect, but the hands of man must be put to *something* before that *something* can be blessed! *"Faith without works is dead"* (James 2:17).

Scene three is an intensely massive rainstorm. Water gushes forth from above and below. Water, as far as the eye can see. The great flood has come. But Noah's ark is stable and steady in the midst of the wind and the waves. He has finished *faith's work* and *faith's work* is working. Faith without works is dead. How explicitly this exhibit demonstrates that truth. Without the work of building the ark, no matter how divine the blueprints were, in this scene Noah would simply be another dead man and the human race extinct.

Can you "see" this truth revealed in the exhibit of *faith's work*? God has given you divine blueprints for abundant life. The *product* of those blueprints will keep you afloat. But the blueprints alone will not float you. It is the *product of the blueprints* that will keep you afloat.

This answers some of the 'why' questions. "Why isn't it working? Why doesn't God come through for me? Why don't I see the manifestation?" Here is why. Some people are trying to stay afloat on paper. They haven't figured out that the paper is just the design from which they are to build the product, and not the product itself. Faith builds! Faith works! Faith acts! Faith searches for a job in order to produce prosperity. Faith chooses habits of health to promote healing. This is a 'working' exhibit. Noah is 'in action'. *Enduring faith* motivates us to manifest *faith's work*.

Faith's Obedience

In exhibit #4, "Faith's Obedience", we see God with Abraham, the father of faith. God speaks to Abraham, *"Go forth from your country, and from your relatives and from your father's house, to the land which I will show you"* (Genesis 12:1).

In scene two, Abraham, all packed up, departs from Haran, his own country, his own house, and his own relatives. He doesn't have a map. He doesn't have a guide. He doesn't even have a compass. All he has is a promise; *"To the land which I will show you!"* What does faith do? *Faith obeys!* Faith obeys even when it cannot see the road ahead. Faith obeys even when it doesn't know the future. Faith demonstrates itself by beginning a journey with no known destination on this earth. Faith accepts the call to a new life and a new land.

Scene three looks a bit tumultuous! There is a struggle going on between Abraham's servants and his nephew Lot's servants (Genesis 13:6-7). Apparently the possessions of Abraham and his nephew are so great the land cannot sustain it all. They are fighting over grazing rights. Abraham and Lot are talking, working out a deal. Abraham allows Lot to choose the best of their lands. Abraham, what did you do? Didn't God say, *"Go forth from your relatives"*? Did you take someone along you weren't supposed to? It looks like you're spending some time babysitting your nephew and negotiating with him.

In scene four a messenger runs toward Abraham. He gasps, "Your relative, Lot, has been taken captive in a war involving nine kings and all his possessions have been stolen." Abraham, wasting no time, calls his servants and assembles his trained men. There are over 300 in Abraham's small army. At Abraham's command they depart in pursuit of Lot's captors.

At nightfall Abraham divides his forces and attacks. The enemy armies, commanded by five kings, are being defeated by this small army of servants led by a man of enduring faith. It is an incredible and valiant victory.

Abraham's men are gathering all the stolen possessions of Sodom and Gomorrah. They gather the rescued women and other people and are taking the possessions back to Sodom and Gomorrah. Lot and his possessions are among them (Genesis 14:13-16).

Melchizedek, the king of Salem, intercepts Abraham. He is a priest of God Most High. He gives bread and wine to Abraham.

Abraham receives it and Melchizedek blesses Abraham. Abraham divides the spoils of war, turning over a tenth of everything to Melchizedek the priest of God (Genesis 14:18-20). Abraham knows where his victory came from. But would he have had this fight if he had departed from *all* his relatives at God's command? What would his exploits be had he not been obliged to rescue his tag-along nephew?

Abraham demonstrates *faith's obedience* and receives these words from the Master Architect and Builder, *"By faith Abraham, when he was called, obeyed by going out to a place which he was to receive for an inheritance; and he went out, not knowing where he was going. By faith he lived as an alien in the land of promise, as in a foreign land, dwelling in tents with Isaac and Jacob, fellow heirs of the same promise; for he was looking for the city which has foundations, whose architect and builder is God"* (Hebrews 11:8-10). By faith Abraham obeyed. But the Master Architect designed the exhibit to display the difficulties Abraham encounters by *including* a relative in his departure *from* his relatives. This may be a minor detail, but it is one that is telling. Could Abraham's lack of attention to the specifics account for the troubles he encountered with Pharaoh in Egypt (Genesis 12:11-20), the difficulties he produced by sleeping with Hagar (Genesis 16:1-12, 21:9-20), and the dilemma he caused Abimelech, king of Gerar (Genesis 20)? The Master Architect uses Abraham as an example to demonstrate for us *faith's obedience*, but He might also be showing us that when faith obeys, paying attention to the specifics, it can save us a boatload of trouble.

Faith's Reckoning

Here we are at exhibit #5 titled "Faith's Reckoning". In scene one an old woman prepares a nursery. She acts like an excited soon-to-be grandmother. Scene two flashes back to one month earlier. God once again speaks to Abraham, *"As for Sarai your wife, you shall not call her name Sarai, but Sarah shall be her name. I will bless her, and indeed I will give you a son by her. Then I will bless her, and she shall be a mother of nations; kings of peoples will come from her"* (Genesis 17:15-16). Abraham is laughing! He is laughing so hard that he cannot stand. He is mumbling to himself, *"Will a child be born to a man one hundred years old? And will Sarah, who is ninety years old, bear a child?"* God responds to Abraham's laughter, *"Sarah your wife will bear you a son, and you shall call his name Isaac; and I will establish My covenant with him for an everlasting covenant for his descendants after him. I will surely return to you at this time next year; and behold, Sarah your wife shall have a son"* (Genesis 17:19, 18:10).

Abraham's wife Sarah is behind him listening at the door of her tent. She laughs, just like Abraham did. She too mumbles something to herself. *"After I have become old, shall I have pleasure, my lord being old also?"* God responds to Abraham, *"Why did Sarah laugh, saying, 'Shall I indeed bear a child, when I am so old?' Is anything too difficult for the LORD? At the appointed time I will return to you, at this time next year, and Sarah will have a son."* Sarah looks afraid and speaks, *"I did not laugh."* God responds to her, *"No, but you did laugh"* (Genesis 18:12-15). That is the end of scene two. The sign simply states, *'Abraham and Sarah were old, advanced in age; Sarah was past childbearing.'* We would guess that with him at 100 and her at 90. What does this have to do with faith's reckoning? Neither one of these parents-to-be seem to reckon that a child will be born. What can two people laughing at God's word teach us about enduring faith?

Scene three takes us back to the old woman working in the nursery. It is Sarah, Abraham's wife. This is *her* nursery, in *her* tent. She is not an excited soon-to-be *grandmother*, she is an excited soon-to-be *mother*. Sarah prepares for the child God promised *her*, a son by the looks of things. She does this even though she has no evidence, aside from the promise, that Isaac is on the way. Look at her making clothes for him, preparing a cradle, and getting his room ready. This ninety-year-old woman must be reckoning that the God who created this world can and will revive the fertility of her aged womb. Sometime in the last month she must have turned her laughter into faith. She must now truly reckon or believe the promise to be a reality. Her actions reveal that she considers as reality, regards as already being, the things that were spoken to her by Him who is faithful. What does faith do? *Faith reckons!* Faith reckons that what God says is already a fact before the evidence is there.

Look into this exhibit at Sarah. She is not pregnant. As excited and vibrant as she is right now, it is evident this lady has not experienced ovulation in years. And yet here she is, getting ready to give birth to a son. Based on what? Only on what she reckons to be so. Faith reckons that what God says is so, *is so,* before *any* evidence (other than His Word) is there to prove it. This is a quiet scene, very serene, and yet it shouts of *power*. It screams of *victory*. Life-giving victory is produced by *faith's reckoning.*

The Master Architect wants us to know that we will encounter episodes of doubt. But if we are willing to employ the power of *faith's reckoning* and begin to act accordingly, we can turn our laughter into the ability to conceive and bring to manifestation what faith reckons to be so. The sign at the exit of this exhibit reads, *"By faith even Sarah herself received ability to conceive, even beyond the proper time of life, since she considered Him faithful who had promised"* (Hebrews 11:11).

Chapter 8

FAITH'S TEST, MATERIAL BLESSING, TRIBAL BLESSING, AND AUTHORITY

Faith's Test

As we read the next part of Abraham's story, we find ourselves declaring, "What is this? Abraham! What are you doing? Isaac is the promised seed! What is Isaac doing on the altar? How could you be sacrificing the very promise you have believed in for over 30 years"?

In the face of this confusion, let's look back at this exhibit's title: "Faith's Test". Now we understand. This is a test. Abraham is taking a test. Abraham tells God that he believes God will raise Isaac from the dead if Abraham kills him. Abraham is willing to sacrifice the manifestation of God's promise to him, because he believes more strongly in the promise than he does the manifestation of the promise.

With a firebrand in one hand and a knife in the other Abraham raises the knife over his bound son. It appears he is going to kill Isaac and offer him as a burnt offering! *"Abraham!"* He hears a voice coming from heaven, *"Abraham! Do not stretch out your hand against the lad, and do nothing to him; for now I know that you fear God, since you have not withheld your son, your only son, from Me"* (Genesis 22:11-12).

Abraham lowers the knife. He spots a ram caught by its horns in the thicket. He cuts Isaac loose and together they walk over to the ram. Abraham slits the ram's throat and sacrifices it on the altar in place of his son Isaac.

This is a single scene exhibit, yet it reveals more about enduring faith than many of the multi-scene exhibits. The sign at the end of the exhibit reads, *"By faith Abraham, when he was tested, offered up Isaac, and he who had received the promises was offering up his only begotten son; it was he to whom it was said, 'In Isaac your descendants shall be called.' He considered that God is able to raise people even from the dead, from which he also received him back as a type"* (Hebrews 11:17-19).

Faith's test is profound. The real test of enduring faith is whether or not we believe more strongly in the promise–in God's Word–than we do in the manifestation of that promise. What is more important in Abraham's life? Is it Isaac, the evidence of God's promise, or God's promise itself? Abraham passed faith's test. Will we? Are we willing to let go of what God has given us, knowing that He will restore it unto us immeasurably? Or do we say, "God, now that I have it, I cannot let it go. The manifestation of Your promise is more important to me than Your promise." This is faith's test.

What will you choose to hold onto: God's promise or the manifestation of that promise? Faith always chooses God's Word over its manifestation enabling you to pass faith's test.

Faith's Material Blessing

At the entrance of exhibit #7, "Faith's Material Blessing", the sign reads *"By faith Isaac blessed Jacob and Esau, even regarding things to come"* (Hebrews 11:20). In scene one, Isaac's wife Rebekah frantically speaks to her son Jacob, *"Behold, I heard your father speak to your brother Esau, saying, 'Bring me some game and prepare a savory dish for me, that I may eat, and bless you in the presence of the LORD before my death.' Now therefore, my son, listen to me as I command you. Go now to the flock and bring me two choice young goats from there, that I may prepare them as a savory dish for your father, such as he loves. Then you shall bring it to your father, that he may eat, so that he may bless you before his death"* (Gen. 27:6-10). Jacob replies, *"Behold, Esau my brother is a hairy man and I am a smooth man. Perhaps my father will feel me, then I will be as a deceiver in his sight, and I will bring upon myself a curse and not a blessing."* Rebekah responds to Jacob's hesitation, *"Your curse be on me, my son; only obey my voice, and go, get them for me"* (Gen. 27:11-13). Faith's Material Blessing exhibit is opening with a scene of duplicity in the making.

In scene two, Rebekah rushes between cooking and sewing. She has Isaac's favorite savory meat on the fire. She cuts and stitches the skins of the goats Jacob brought her. Jacob watches apprehensively. She sorts through her oldest son Esau's clothing, selects a garment and places it on Jacob. She puts the goatskin she was sewing on his hands and his neck. This plan of deception is unfolding right in the middle of Faith's Hall of Fame. How can faith's material blessing come from this? The food is cooked and

61

Rebekah gives Jacob the bread and meat to take to his father. The tension of deception is in the air.

In scene three Jacob enters his father Isaac's tent saying, *"My father."* Isaac responds, *"Here I am. Who are you, my son?"* Jacob replies, *"I am Esau, your first-born; I have done as you have told me. Get up, please, sit and eat of my game, that you may bless me"* (Gen. 27:18-19). Isaac seems surprised, *"How is it that you have it so quickly my son?"* Jacob hesitates slightly, *"Because the Lord your God caused it to happen to me"* (Gen. 27:20). How daring this falsehood of Jacob to name God as his source of a quick kill. But Isaac doesn't know what to think. A look of confusion is on his face. He speaks, *"Please come close that I may feel you, my son, whether you are really my son Esau or not."* Jacob moves closer to his father. Isaac touches Jacob. *"The voice is the voice of Jacob, but the hands are the hands of Esau"* Isaacs says, *"Are you really my son Esau"* (Gen. 27:21, 24)? Will Jacob come clean? Jacob replies, *"I am."*. No, the deceiver is taking this all the way to his goal.

In scene four Jacob moves closer and kisses his father at his father's request. Isaac smells the garments of Esau that Jacob is wearing and now seems convinced. Isaac speaks a blessing to Jacob saying, *"See, the smell of my son is like the smell of a field which the LORD has blessed; Now may God give you of the dew of heaven, And of the fatness of the earth, And an abundance of grain and new wine; May peoples serve you, And nations bow down to you; Be master of your brothers, And may your mother's sons bow down to you. Cursed be those who curse you, And blessed be those who bless you"* (Gen. 27:27-29).

Isaac blesses Jacob with *faith's material blessing*, but he thinks it is Esau. Listen to faith speak; listen to the power of prophetic faith, even when spoken in circumstances of false pretense. Under false pretense Jacob was blessed with *faith's material blessing*; the dew of heaven, the fatness of the earth, an abundance of grain, plenty of wine, and the authority of leadership roles. The sign on scene four reads, *"So the man became exceedingly prosperous, and had large flocks and female and male servants and camels and donkeys"* (Genesis 30:43).

This should loosen our tongues and lessen our concern over making a mistake. Here a man of God is being deceived and yet, by faith, pronounces a blessing of fatness, abundance, and authority over a man of whom it shall come to pass. *Faith's material blessing* is evidenced in this exhibit.

As we look back down the hall from where we've come, there seems to be a progression in the manifestations of faith. It appears that *faith's worship* is what moves us into *faith's walk.* And *faith's walk* motivates us to manifest *faith's work. Faith's work* then implants a desire to demonstrate *faith's obedience. Faith's obedience* will elicit a *faith inspired reckoning, which prepares us for faith's test*! Having passed *faith's test* we are then ready to receive the *material blessings of faith* demonstrated in exhibit #7.

Many ask, "Why haven't I experienced faith's material blessings?" The answer *may* lie in the fact that they have not experienced faith's worship, walk, work, obedience, or reckoning! It *may* lie in the fact that they have not passed faith's test!

Faith's Hall of Fame is an exhibit of faith's witnesses. God, being a God of order, placed these witnesses in a progressive order to demonstrate the steps and balance of a biblical faith walk.

We would do well to lay aside the '3 step faith formula for walking in financial freedom' and pick up God's 'Manufacturer's Handbook'. Then turn to the chapter on 'How to Experience a Lifetime Journey of Enduring Faith' and begin where the Manufacturer tells us to begin. We are trying to get on the faith ladder, halfway up and wondering why it is so difficult, why we can't seem to reach it. We must start with the first rung of faith, faith's worship. When the Manufacturer's Handbook is followed, *faith's material blessing* comes easy, so easy it doesn't even need to be done right, as exhibit #7 demonstrates to us. What does faith do? Regardless of the circumstances, it speaks *faith's material blessing*!

Faith's Tribal Blessing

In exhibit #8, "Faith's Tribal Blessing", we find Jacob, who received faith's material blessing, manifesting faith's tribal blessing. The entrance sign reads, *"By faith Jacob, as he was dying, blessed each of the sons of Joseph, and worshiped, leaning on the top of his staff"* (Hebrews 11:20). In this exhibit we find Jacob lying on his bed. His son Joseph enters and Jacob lifts himself, sitting up on the bed. He speaks to Joseph, *"Now your two sons, who were born to you in the land of Egypt before I came to you in Egypt, are mine; Ephraim and Manasseh shall be mine, as Reuben and Simeon are"* (Genesis 48:5). Jacob just adopted his grandsons and elevated them to the status of his own sons, even his first-born. This qualifies them to receive a double inheritance. Jacob speaks again, *"Bring them to me, please, that I may bless them"* (Gen. 48:9). Joseph motions for his sons to come to their grand-father. They sit on Jacob's knees. He kisses and embraces them.

Joseph then moves Ephraim from Jacob's left knee and Manasseh to Jacob's right to receive the tribal blessing of the first-born. But Jacob is crossing his hands, placing his right on Ephraim's head and his left on Manasseh, the first-born. He speaks, *"Bless the lads; and may my name live on in them, and the names of my fathers Abraham and Isaac; and may they grow into a multitude in the midst of the earth"* (Gen. 48:16).

Joseph is displeased. He grasps his father's right hand and moves it to Manasseh's head saying, *"Not so, my father, for this one is the first-born. Place your right hand on his head,"* Jacob refuses to comply. He speaks, *"I know, my son, I know; he also will become a people and he also will be great. However, his younger brother shall be greater than he, and his descendants shall become a multitude of nations."* Jacob once again crosses his hands and continues, *"By you Israel will pronounce blessing, saying, 'May God make you like Ephraim and Manasseh'"* (Gen. 48:18-20). Jacob has just placed Ephraim before Manasseh. In the same way God chose Isaac over first-born Ishmael, Jacob over first-born Esau, and Joseph over first-born Reuben, He now sets Ephraim over Manasseh through faith's tribal blessing.

Jacob turns to Joseph, *"Behold, I am about to die, but God will be with you, and bring you back to the land of your fathers. I give you one portion more than your brothers, which I took from the hand of the Amorite with my sword and my bow"* (Gen. 48:21). By giving Joseph double inheritance, Jacob has just sealed the transfer of first-born rights from Reuben to Joseph.

This is a picture of God taking us as His own. We see our "new Father" adopting us and giving us the inheritance along with His own Son. We are part of the tribe. We belong.

But what does this exhibit demonstrate about enduring faith? First, we see that faith manifests itself prophetically. We see a father speaking prophetically over the lives of his sons. To emulate Jacob we would speak prophetically over our sons and daughters. We would prophesy of their place in the kingdom. We would speak of the godly things that they will pursue. We would help them "see" themselves worshipping God, walking hand in hand with Him, working with Him, obeying Him, reckoning or speaking His word as though it were so, and passing faith's tests. We would speak to them as part of the tribe, even when they weren't acting like it. We would be their "faith eyes" until they developed their own.

Some "sons" were by-passed and the birthright blessing passed on to, not only a younger brother, but to grandchildren as well. What does enduring faith do? Enduring faith doesn't give up! Faith doesn't quit! If you miss it with your sons, if you've got a Reuben, a Simeon, or a Judah, grab hold of that grandson or granddaughter and pass on the legacy of enduring faith. You may have come to know the things of God after your children were grown, but that doesn't deprive you of an opportunity to leave a legacy of faith. Transfer the *tribal blessing* of enduring faith. No grandchildren? No excuse! Nieces, nephews, or neighbors; find someone in the succeeding generations to speak the blessing of enduring faith into. It's not too late and it's not time to retire. Don't give up! If you need to skip a generation to get the job done, do it. Whatever you need to do to leave a legacy, do it – do it by faith! *"How beautiful are the feet of those who bring glad tidings of good things"* (Isaiah 52:7). What does faith do? *Faith speaks the tribal blessing!* Speak the glad tidings of *faith's tribal blessing* over a child. If not your own, then your son's or your daughter's. If not theirs, someone's.

Before we move on from this exhibit, let's reflect once again on the progression of these manifestations of faith. Even here, with the *seemingly simple* manifestation of faith's tribal blessing, it is rarely seen, historically or currently, in men or women who have not experienced faith's worship, walk, work, obedience, reckoning, or test. It appears that the men and women who have endured through at least several of these manifestations are much more likely to manifest *faith's tribal blessing* over the succeeding generations. Having trouble with this one? Go back to exhibit #1 and start with faith's worship.

Faith's Authority

In exhibit #9, "Faith's Authority", we hear Joseph, faith's tribal blessing recipient, demonstrating faith's authority as he speaks to his brothers. *"I am about to die, but God will surely take care of you and bring you up from this land to the land which He promised on oath to Abraham, to Isaac and to Jacob"* (Gen. 50:24). He makes them promise him something. *"God will surely take care of you, and you shall carry my bones up from here"* (Gen. 50:25).

Enduring faith speaks with authority. Joseph speaks with absolute assurance and authority regarding the promises of God. He says, *"God will surely take care of you..."* What does faith do? *Faith speaks with authority regarding the promises of God.* There is no equivocation in Joseph's statements about what God is going to do. He knows. He has heard the Word and he knows. This is a simple exhibit, no tools, no machines, no construction, no altars, no translations, not even an old lady preparing a nursery; just a dying man on a bed speaking to his brothers. But the power and authority behind those words echo up and down the halls of this museum, *because those words echo the Words of God.*

To emulate Joseph, speak the Words that God has spoken to you, His promises, with such authority and such assurance, that it echoes throughout our homes, echoes through the halls of our schools, echoes above the noise of the machines in our factories, and most assuredly echoes in those great halls that we call churches. But sad to say this is not what we see. The truth be told, we see more equivocation regarding the promises of God in the church than we do anywhere else. The reverberation of all the things God doesn't do, won't do, no longer will do, and can't do drowns out any echoing voice of authority stating what God *will most surely* do! Why is this?

It is a lack of enduring faith. *Enduring faith keeps "seeing" when things can't be seen.* Short term, impatient, intellectual faith quits when it doesn't see things that can't be seen. So excuses arise. Promises are spiritualized, categorized, dispensationalized, penalized, and exorcised of their power. The *one* place where God's promises should authoritatively be echoing off the walls has turned into something that sounds like a political nominating convention. And all because we have forgotten one simple, very simple truth; *"We walk by faith, not by sight"* (2 Cor. 5:7). God said, *"The righteous will live by his faith"* (Hab. 2:4).

Joseph had no visible evidence that Israel would ever possess their land. What he had was a promise from God, and upon that promise and that alone did he speak with authority and assurance that it was as good as done. *"You shall carry my bones up from here"* (Genesis 50:25). Emulate this witness. Begin to speak the promises with authority and assurance. Speak them in your home. Speak them at school. Speak them at work. And of all places, speak them in your church. Speak them as though they are as good as done. *Say what God says you have whether or not you see what He says you have. Enduring faith in God and His Word is what gains approval, not whether you see or feel the physical reality of His promises.* It was good enough for Joseph to have his bones experience the promise. That alone was enough to keep him speaking the promise.

I'm looking for the city which has foundations, whose builder and architect is God. I'm seeking a country of my own, a better country, a heavenly one. That alone is enough to keep me speaking the promises of God with authority and assurance regardless of whether or not I ever experience even one of them on this earth. When I arrive at that heavenly country, I want it to be said that I, one of His righteous ones, walked by faith and not by sight. I want God to say, "Son, you believed what I said, you spoke what I spoke, and you acted like it was true when everything appeared contrary to it. Well done, my faith walkin' son, well done!"

The men of this earth can say what they want. They can accuse me of adhering to a "name it and claim it, blab it and grab it" gospel. They can say that I'm deceived, that I'm in denial. They can question my motives and call it selfishness. I don't care. All I care about is that on that day I hear Him say, "You were like Me, son, calling things that were not as though they were. You were in agreement with Me. You talked like Me, seeing into the future. You walked by faith, pleasing Me." That is what I want to hear. I'll take seventy years of ridicule here; just give me eternity to hear my Father say that.

The sign at the exit of this simple single-scene exhibit reads, *"By faith Joseph, when he was dying, made mention of the exodus of the sons of Israel, and gave orders concerning his bones"* (Hebrews 11:22). Joseph *gave orders* concerning his bones. What does faith do? *Faith speaks with authority.* As we leave this exhibit demonstrating *faith's authority*, once again looking at the progression of faith, it is seldom that one hears *faith's authority* spoken, in heartfelt sincerity, by one who has not experienced many of the manifestations of faith that we have seen in this hall so far. Are you having trouble speaking with *faith's authority*? Start with *faith's worship.*

Chapter 9

FAITH'S RECOGNITION AND DECLARATION

Faith's Recognition

Exhibit #10 is "Faith's Recognition." The sign at the entrance reads, *"By faith Moses' parents hid him for three months after he was born, because they saw he was no ordinary child, and they were not afraid of the king's edict"* (Hebrews 11:23).

Amram and Jochebed, Moses' parents, hide him, rebelling against the king of Egypt and his edict to kill all Hebrew males at birth. They heard from God. Faith has come and manifested itself in recognition, recognition that the call of God is on the life of their son. This manifestation of faith has moved them to circumvent the plans of the enemy to destroy God's man. For three months they have attempted to keep this baby quiet and hidden.

Now what are they doing here in scene two? They discuss a plan. But they talk as though it is not a plan of their own. They speak of a *divine* plan, a *divine* strategy. They are making references to Noah's divine plans we viewed in exhibit #3. Like Noah, it sounds as though they're going to build an ark to save their own family. Jochebed looks shocked, but Amram laughs as he explains to her that it will be much, much smaller than Noah's and heads to his shop. Jochebed laughs now as she opens a trunk by the wall. She lifts a wicker basket from the trunk and places it on the table. Amram returns with a bucket of tar and pitch. They work together to cover the basket with tar and pitch. Pleased with the results, Amram suggests a test fit and Jochebed places Moses in the basket.

In scene three Amram and Jochebed are on the bank of the Nile River. They have Moses in the basket. Amram explains to his wife that the reeds in front of them are near the place where Pharaoh's daughter bathes. Together they place the basket in the reeds. As they leave, they give Moses' sister Miriam charge over him and his little ark to find out what will happen. They have heard from God. They believe God. They are following the divine plan and it is now out of their hands.

Pharaoh's daughter, Thermuthis, and her maidens walk along the riverbank. She spots the basket containing Moses and sends her maid to bring it to her. She opens the basket. *"This is one of the Hebrew's children."* she tells her maid (Ex. 2:6). Miriam approaches her, *"Shall I go and call a nurse for you from the Hebrew women that she may nurse the child for you?"* Thermuthis responds, *"Go ahead"* (Exodus 2:7-8) and Miriam rushes off to get her mother.

In scene four Jochebed arrives at the river. Thermuthis talks with her concerning nursing, care, instructions, and protection. *"Take this child away and nurse him for me and I will give you your wages"*(Exodus 2:9). This divine plan includes Pharaoh's daughter falling in love with baby Moses and offering to pay his own mother to nurse him. A child condemned to death by a king's edict being cared for by his own mother but at the expense of the very author of that edict. Surely God has a sense of humor.

This is what *faith's recognition* can bring to pass. Not only will it thwart the enemy's plans, but actually use his servants to facilitate the process. In this exhibit Jochebed not only can care for her own child but gets wages to nurse her own son from the very people he is going to grow up to defeat.

It is so interesting to examine the witnesses who followed the divine plan of *faith's recognition* and see the outcome. We could do the same with the parents or guardians of Joseph, Samuel, Samson, Esther, John the Baptist and Jesus. But to emulate these witnesses' enduring faith is to throw caution to the wind and say, "God, whatever You show me, I will do." These witnesses of *faith's recognition* didn't fear ridicule, punishment, or even death. They all laid self aside and poured themselves into, and even sacrificed, the object of *faith's recognition*.

Amram and Jochebed did not fear the king's edict, but defied it, and then sacrificed their fatherhood and motherhood of Moses. Elkanah and Hannah did the same with their son Samuel, turning him over to the Lord under the supervision of Eli the priest, after he was weaned (1 Sam. 1). Menoah and his wife followed the divine plan for God's man, their son Samson, by altering their lifestyles to accommodate the plan for his (Judges 13). Mordecai took in Esther, his uncle's daughter, as his own and recognized the call on her life to save his people from destruction (Esther 2:7-11). He encouraged, even exhorted, her to rise up to the call on her life, which could potentially bring her death (Esther 4:13-14).

What about Zacharias and Elizabeth in Luke 1? Who knows what they had to put up with in the object of their *faith's recognition*. With their age and the disposition of their son John, it is very likely hurtful and humiliating comments were elicited. Consider Joseph and Mary. We need not even comment on this manifestation of *faith's recognition*. No one in this world can even begin to imagine what it must have been like to recognize and know what their faith recognized.

This manifestation of faith brings both exhilaration and pain. The exhilaration comes with the recognition that God's hand is upon the life of an individual. But when the hand of God draws that individual toward their destiny, it oftentimes takes them to places of separation and hardship. When you are close to the individual, and begin recognizing the path toward their destination, seeing the required *shaping* that is taking place on the journey to that destination brings heartache.

Mary, the mother of Jesus, is the ultimate example of this. Imagine the exhilaration in her heart as she recognizes, in her Son, the Messiah, the Savior of the world. But then, imagine the heart wrenching pain of seeing that same Son, tortured and crucified, on the journey toward His destination. At this point you might say, "I'm not so sure I want to emulate the witnesses in this exhibit." Let me say this. Everyone who has ever experienced the manifestation of faith's recognition would gladly go through it all again, because the exhilaration of being a part of God's hand in *faith's recognition* far outweighs the pain experienced in viewing the journey.

Notice that the manifestations of faith are progressively becoming more challenging to the natural mind. Notice that each exhibit requires one to enter into a deeper walk spiritually and a shallower walk sensually. If one is to emulate the journey of these witnesses, then one must learn to absolve oneself from sense realm thinking. One cannot walk this journey living by the senses. Spirit realm thinking is required to pass through the pain and heartache of the natural realm journey. Without spirit realm thinking one will not choose *faith's recognition*, but instead will fight against it. Without spirit realm thinking one will not choose to take *faith's test*. Without spirit realm thinking, one will not choose *faith's obedience*. And an unwillingness to choose one of faith's manifestations will hinder one from choosing the next.

By the time we get to the final exhibit, *"faith's consummation"*, you will see that the faith required for this manifestation can only come from having experienced and walked in many of the manifestations of faith's preceding exhibits. So choose *faith's recognition*. Look into the lives of those close to you and see if the hand of God is upon them. If you recognize it, nurture them, guide them, and prepare them for what most likely lies ahead. Then prepare yourself. Prepare yourself for the separation when the call is implemented. Prepare yourself for the pain when they are criticized. Prepare yourself for the hurt when they stumble. Prepare yourself for the agony when they are rejected. Mary would most surely tell you that it is worth it.

Faith's Declaration

"Faith's Declaration" is demonstrated in exhibit #11. The witness demonstrating *faith's declaration* is the product of *faith's recognition*. Moses is grown up and demonstrating *faith's declaration* for us. Listen to him; he refuses to be called the son of Pharaoh's daughter. He declares his non-candidacy for the kingship of Egypt. His declaration is, "I'm not running for office. I'm not looking for position. I'm not interested in a title, and I don't want power." Like Abraham he sees Jesus Christ (Jn. 8:56). As Abraham saw the day of Jesus Christ, so Moses now sees it also (Heb. 11:26). The sign at this opening scene reads, *"By faith Moses, when he had grown up, refused to be called the son of Pharaoh's daughter; choosing rather to endure ill-treatment with the people of God than to enjoy the passing pleasures of sin, considering the reproach of Christ greater riches than the treasures of Egypt; for he was looking to the reward"* (Hebrews 11:24-26**).**

In scene two Moses considers the reproach of Christ greater riches than the treasures of Egypt, than kingship, than title, prestige, or power. He states *that* as the reason he is *"going out to his brethren."* He is on a mission. He spots an Egyptian beating one of his Hebrew brothers. He follows the offending Egyptian. He looks around and seeing no one else, Moses avenges the beating of his Hebrew brother. He strikes him down and buries the body in the sand (Ex. 1:11-12). This heroic feat, if found out, should rally his brethren around him.

The following day, as seen in scene three, Moses happens upon two Hebrews fighting. He is addressing the aggressor, *"Why are you striking your companion?"* The Hebrew answers, *"Who made you a prince or a judge over us? Are you intending to kill me as you killed the Egyptian?"* Fear crosses Moses face as he realizes his secret has been found out, *"Surely the matter has become known"* (Exodus 2:13-14). Apparently Moses is not ready to lead, and his people are not ready to be led. Killing the Egyptian must not have been God's way. Moses will need to find a new strategy.

And his people, who are more interested in fighting each other than their captors, will need to learn to unite.

How sad when men with a common enemy fight against each other. Let us not emulate their behavior. Let us emulate Moses' behavior in making *faith's declaration*. Let us speak *faith's declaration* and renounce our son-ship to the world. Let us choose to endure ill treatment, wrong, hurt, even injury with the people of God instead of the passing pleasures of sin. Let us declare that we esteem the reproach of Christ as greater riches than anything this world has to offer us. Let us emulate Moses' faith eyes, seeing far into the future, and declare our reward, our son-ship, our king-ship, in a better country, that is, a heavenly one.

What does faith do? Faith declares that the *riches* of the unseen realm are greater than the foundationless positions and titles of this world. Moses pre-empted God's plan by killing this Egyptian, but it was not position that Moses sought; it was presence, God's presence. If Moses wanted position, he'd have stayed in the palace. It was God's presence he desired.

Scene four takes us forty years into the future. The sign reads, *"After forty years had passed, an angel appeared to Moses in the flames of a burning bush in the desert near Mount Sinai"* (Acts 7:30). Moses has been in this wilderness, forty years in his personal wilderness, seeking God's presence. Faith's declaration has brought Moses to this place, and it is in this place that we see the manifestation of God's presence. Look at that bush, burning with fire, and yet the bush is not consumed! Listen as God speaks, *"Moses, Moses."* Moses answers, *"Here I am"* (Ex. 3:4). God explains to Moses that He is now going to use him to deliver the Hebrews from Egyptian bondage and take them to the Promised

Land. Moses balks, *"Who am I?"* he asks. Forty years ago this guy would have volunteered. Self-confidence and self-conceit ruled. He thought he knew what he could do back then. He knows now that his own wisdom and power will not suffice.

"Certainly I will be with you," God says. Moses asks God, *"What do I tell the sons of Israel your name is"* (Ex. 3:13-14)? Listen to what God tells him. "Take them a blank check." Did you hear that? God said, "Take them a blank check. Moses, tell them *I AM!* Tell them *I AM* has sent you. What do they need? *I AM!* What do they want? *I AM!* What do they desire? *I AM!* Give them a blank check, Moses, for *I AM* their need. *I AM* their want. *I AM* their desire. Give them a blank check!"

What is this? This is all preparation for the manifestation of *faith's fearlessness.* Faith's declaration takes us to a place where we can experience faith's fearlessness. *Faith's declaration* is a precedent to faith's fearlessness. Moses is in preparation.

Chapter 10

FAITH'S FEARLESSNESS, PROTECTION, AND PRESERVATION

Faith's Fearlessness

Exhibit #12 demonstrates "Faith's Fearlessness". In scene one, we find Moses conversing with God. *"What if they will not believe me or listen to what I say? For they may say, 'The LORD has not appeared to you,'"* Moses says. *"What is that in your hand?"* God asks. *"A staff,"* Moses replies. *"Throw it on the ground,"* God says. Moses throws it down. It turns into a snake. Moses runs from it. God tells Moses to stop running. *"Stretch out your hand and grasp it by its tail"* (Ex. 4:1-4). Moses reaches for it and grabs it by its tail. What risk, grabbing a snake by its tail. But now, it has become a staff again. The staff is different somehow; it now appears that it is *the staff of God.* It's the anointing: God's power. Moses has the anointing, God's power, in his hand.

God speaks again, *"that they may believe that the LORD, the God of their fathers, the God of Abraham, the God of Isaac, and the God of Jacob, has appeared to you."* Moses looks at Him, not quite certain. God continues, *"Now put your hand into your bosom."*

Moses puts his hand into his bosom. He takes it out and his hand is leprous like snow. *"Put your hand into your bosom again,"* God says. Moses places his hand into his bosom again. He pulls it out. It is exactly like the rest of his flesh!

"If they will not believe you or heed the witness of the first sign, they may believe the witness of the last sign," God tells Moses. *"But if they will not believe even these two signs or heed what you say, then you shall take some water from the Nile and pour it on the dry ground; and the water which you take from the Nile will become blood on the dry ground"* (Ex. 4:5-9).

God is building the foundation for faith's fearlessness into Moses. *"You shall take in your hand this staff, with which you shall perform the signs"* are God's final words to Moses in this first scene.

In scene two Moses and Aaron stand before Pharaoh saying, *"Thus says the LORD, the God of Israel, 'Let My people go that they may celebrate a feast to Me in the wilderness.'"* Pharaoh responds, *"Who is the LORD that I should obey His voice to let Israel go? I do not know the LORD, and besides, I will not let Israel go"* (Ex. 5:1-2). Moses does not back down. He displays fearlessness as he confronts Pharaoh. *"The God of the Hebrews has met with us,"* Moses adamantly declares. Pharaoh is angry and sends them away, *"Moses and Aaron, why do you draw the people away from their work? Get back to your labors"* (Ex. 5:4).

Scene three, in another confrontation with Pharaoh, Pharaoh questions the validity of Moses' claims. *"Work a miracle,"* he demands. Fearless, Moses turns to Aaron, *"Take your staff and throw it down before Pharaoh, that it may become a serpent"* (Ex. 7:9). Aaron tosses his staff on the floor. It turns into a serpent.

80

Pharaoh calls for his wise men and sorcerers, the magicians of Egypt. All of them throw their staffs on the floor and the staffs turn into serpents. But Aaron's staff turned serpent swallows up all the other serpents. The sign at the end of this scene reads, *"Yet Pharaoh's heart was hardened, and he did not listen to them, as the LORD had said"* (Exodus 7:13).

Scene four takes us into what appears to be a multi-screen theatre-in-the-round. This is incredible, if not a little overwhelming. Moses is on every screen confronting Pharaoh. Look at his fearlessness as he calls forth plague after plague upon the land of Egypt. On screen one, all the water in Egypt turns to blood at Moses' command. On screen two, frogs cover all the land of Egypt, inside and out, after Moses fearlessly calls them forth. Screen three shows the dust of Egypt turning into gnats. On screen four, flies swarm the land of Egypt devouring everything they see. Screen five shows all the livestock in Egypt dropping over dead with disease. Horses, donkeys, camels, sheep, none of the livestock in the field are spared, except for the Israelites' livestock.

On screen six Moses takes silt from a kiln and, standing before Pharaoh, throws it toward the sky. The silt becomes boils breaking out on the Egyptians and what remains of their animals. Screen seven shows a massive amount of hail pouring down over all of Egypt shattering every plant and tree in the land by its force. On screen eight a fearless Moses brings locusts into all the territory of Egypt. They are so thick the land is darkened by their presence and nothing green is left in all the land. Screen nine is dark. Nothing but the voice of Moses fearlessly calling forth darkness over the land, a three day total Egyptian blackout. The only light in all the land is inside the Israelite dwellings. This darkness can be felt. It is so heavy no one can move. The final screen shows a sad but fearless Moses calling forth death on every first-born in the land of Egypt. From the first-born of Pharaoh to the first-born of slave girls, the bodies of children pile up on screen ten. But against the sons of Israel a dog does not even bark.

The sign over this scene reads, *"The LORD gave the people favor in the sight of the Egyptians. Furthermore, the man Moses himself was greatly esteemed in the land of Egypt, both in the sight of Pharaoh's servants and in the sight of the people"* (Exodus 11:3). This fearless leader has taken a people despised as slaves and burdened with labor and turned them into wealthy recipients of favor. So much so that the exit sign states, *"Now the sons of Israel had done according to the word of Moses, for they had requested from the Egyptians articles of silver and articles of gold, and clothing; and the LORD had given the people favor in the sight of the Egyptians, so that they let them have their request. Thus they plundered the Egyptians"* (Exodus 12:35-36). Moses' fearlessness turned the tables on the Israelites' captors making the poor become rich and the rich become poor.

In scene five Moses departs Egypt leading the massive nation of Israel. He displays fearlessness as he embarks with several million people on a journey into the wilderness. The product of *faith's fearlessness* is now being manifested in this exhibit. The sign over this final scene reads, *"By faith he left Egypt, not fearing the wrath of the king; for he endured, as seeing Him who is unseen"* (Hebrews 11:27). Why didn't Moses fear this "visible" king? He was fearless because he saw the Invisible One. Moses endured fearlessly in faith by "seeing' Him who is unseen.

How can we emulate this witness in manifesting *faith's fearlessness*? Someone may argue, "I've never had a burning bush experience." If we are in Christ, we have. We already have what it takes to emulate this witness. We have the anointing, and we have seen the Invisible One (1 Jn. 2:20, 27). The anointing and the Invisible One reside in us. The question we may need to ask, though, is have we gone out into the desert to seek His presence? There is a significant difference between Him being present in you and you being in His presence. Could it be that the reason we are not seeing faith's fearlessness manifested is because we are so busy pursuing *position* instead of *presence*? This manifestation, faith's fearlessness, can only be displayed in our lives, in its reality, after we have spent time in the wilderness seeking the presence of God.

What does enduring faith do? Enduring faith seeks the *presence of God* in order to obtain *faith's fearlessness*. And once again, to obtain the desire to lay aside the pursuit of position, prestige and power for His presence, in order to manifest faith's fearlessness, requires one to have experienced faith's worship, walk, work, obedience, reckoning and test. For this, in itself, is one of faith's tests. A sacrifice is involved. The sacrifice is you. The sacrifice is self.

Faith's Protection

Our tour takes us to exhibit #13, where we see "Faith's Protection" demonstrated. Once again, our faith witness is Moses and the entrance sign reads *"By faith he kept the Passover and the sprinkling of the blood, so that he who destroyed the firstborn would not touch them"* (Hebrews 11:28). This manifestation takes place during the tenth and final plague upon Egypt. Moses is explaining to the people how the blood of the Passover Lamb will be a sign, a token of obedience, for God to see and pass over with His judgment. He tells them, *"You shall take a bunch of hyssop and dip it in the blood which is in the basin, and apply some of the blood that is in the basin to the lintel and the two doorposts; and none of you shall go outside the door of his house until morning"* (Ex. 12:22).

Look at the faith in God's protection demonstrated in Moses' gestures. He is absolutely convinced that the death angel will pass over every Israelite's home that has this "sign" on the lintel. He explains to them how to "apply the blood". He tells them to get their loins girded, sandals on their feet, and staff in their hand, and to eat the Passover Lamb in haste (Ex. 12:11). Moses is excited. God's judgment is going to *Passover* His people.

Do we emulate this kind of passion for the Passover Lamb? Do we have our loins girded with truth? Do we have the sandals of the preparation of the gospel on our feet? Do we have the staff of His Word in our hands? Are we hastily *eating* of the Passover Lamb as though there will be a famine tomorrow? Are we ready to depart at a moments notice? Or have we simply sprinkled the *Blood* on the doorposts of our lives? That alone is enough for judgment to pass over, but if we desire to see *faith's protection* manifested, we must ready ourselves. If we desire to see our *"Egypts"* plundered, we must be prepared to go.

Scene two begins with the people of Israel bowing down and worshipping. As they go to their homes, they do exactly as Moses instructed them. The Israelites eat the Passover Lamb in haste. They are prepared to depart this land of slavery at a moment's notice. They believe this is the day of their salvation. It is midnight. What is that? An eerie feeling is in the air. Listen. It is dogs barking.

No, howling. The dogs of Egypt are penetrating the air with howls of death. They know what is happening. They smell the angel of death. But the dogs of the sons of Israel are silent. They sleep. There is no smell of death in the land of Goshen. Its people smell only victory.

We are hit with the sound of screaming and wailing in scene three. Its sign reads, *"There was a great cry in Egypt, for there was no home where there was not someone dead"* (Exodus 12:30). Pharaoh, agitated, demands Moses and Aaron's presence. When they arrive with his servants he addresses them, *"Rise up, get out from among my people, both you and the sons of Israel; and go, worship the LORD, as you have said. Take both your flocks and your herds, as you have said, and go, and bless me also"* (Exodus 12:31-32). Moses and Aaron depart.

Scene four opens with Moses shouting out commands of departure. They resonate in the air as they are passed through the ranks of this highly organized multitude who have readied themselves to depart from their slavery. Moses tells them, *"Each man ask from his neighbor and each woman from her neighbor for articles of silver and articles of gold"* (Ex. 11:2). They are doing as he instructed, and the Egyptians are complying! Generously! They are urging the Israelites to go in haste as they load them with silver, gold, and clothing. They tell them to go saying, *"We shall all be dead."* What a turn of events for the Israelites on this night demonstrating *faith's protection* for us.

The sign under this scene reads, *"Now the sons of Israel had done according to the word of Moses, for they had requested from the Egyptians articles of silver and articles of gold, and clothing; and the LORD had given the people favor in the sight of the Egyptians, so that they let them have their request. Thus* they plundered the Egyptians" (Exodus 12:35-36). Plundered! The slaves' owners, coming out to Goshen, are offering 400 years of back pay. "Here, you want our silver, our gold? How about our jewels? Take all of our clothes, too. Please, just go!" Plundered! These people of God desired to see their *"Egypt"* plundered, and prepared themselves to go. And they left loaded down with riches. It was a reversal of fortunes for the possessor and the possessed.

If you want to turn the table on the possessor of your bondages and if you want to escape from the enemy's camp and plunder all that he robbed you of at the same time, then you must become as full of faith and passionate as Moses is here in exhibit #13. You must prepare yourself and eat hastily of the Lamb of God. Be ready to depart, for when it is time, it is time. This exhibit's epilogue speaks of freedom with flair, *"The Egyptians urged the people, to send them out of the land in haste, for they said, 'We will all be dead'"* (Exodus 12:33). You get all armored up, looking like God from your helmet to your boots, and the devil will release you from your bondages so quick, you'll think you hear him saying, "Go! Go now! Go in haste!" How do we manifest *faith's protection*? We manifest *faith's protection* by applying the Blood of Jesus and preparing ourselves for departure with passion.

Faith's Preservation

Exhibit #14 reveals "Faith's Preservation". This manifestation is demonstrated not by "a" witness, but by a nation of witnesses under the leadership of two different men, Moses and Joshua. *Faith's preservation* is manifested in the crossing of the Red Sea, *"By faith they passed through the Red Sea as though they were passing through dry land; and the Egyptians, when they attempted it, were drowned"* (Hebrews 11:29).

The exhibit opens with the Israelites at the shore of the Red Sea and the Egyptian Army closing in behind them. The Israelites, very frightened, cry out to the Lord. They shout at Moses, *"Is it because there were no graves in Egypt that you have taken us away to die in the wilderness? Why have you dealt with us in this way, bringing us out of Egypt? Is this not the word that we spoke to you in Egypt, saying, 'Leave us alone that we may serve the Egyptians'? For it would have been better for us to serve the Egyptians than to die in the wilderness"* (Ex. 14:11-12). It sounds like these folks are having trouble "seeing" *faith's preservation.* Moses responds, *"Do not fear! Stand by and see the salvation of the LORD, which He will accomplish for you today; for the Egyptians whom you have seen today, you will never see them again forever. The LORD will fight for you while you keep silent"* (Ex. 14:13-14). Sounds like good advice.

However, in scene two God speaks to Moses, *"Why are you crying out to Me? Tell the sons of Israel to go forward. As for you, lift up your staff and stretch out your hand over the sea and divide it, and the sons of Israel shall go through the midst of the sea on dry land"* (Ex. 14:15-16). What sounded like good advice wasn't. Moving forward, not sitting in silence nor whining to God, initiates faith's preservation.

There is the angel of God, in the pillar of cloud. This is Jehovah Himself, Who has been in front of them all this way. He now goes behind them. He has become darkness to the Egyptians preventing them from approaching the Israelite camp, but at the same time He is lighting the night for the Israelites (Ex. 14:19-20). This must be what Paul meant when he said Christ is the aroma of death to those who are perishing but to those who are being saved, the aroma from Life to life (2 Cor. 2:15-16). It is the same source but two different views.

Look at Moses in scene three with the anointing, the staff of God, lifted up over the sea. He obeys the instructions of *faith's preservation*. Look at the water split! Dry ground, dry ground right there in the middle of the sea. Water congeals into walls 75, 80, maybe 100 feet high, solid ice, thickened by the blast of God's nostrils. There go the Israelites, trucking across like it is some kind of major highway. Incredible! Cruising across the seabed like it is the autobahn. But look! The Egyptians follow them, horses, chariots and all. They must believe in the God of the Israelites, too. This really is "blind faith." With all the flies, frogs, gnats, locusts, darkness, hail, and the death of their firstborn, what else would cause an Egyptian soldier to ride out onto God's highway through the middle of a sea? Would you? No way!

God is doing it. The sign under this scene reads, *"As for Me, behold, I will harden the hearts of the Egyptians so that they will go in after them; and I will be honored through Pharaoh and all his army, through his chariots and his horsemen"* (Ex. 14:17). God entices them to follow. But the wheels of their chariots fall off, really slowing them down. Now this looks more like an LA freeway than the autobahn. The Israelites have arrived at the other shore. As Moses lifts his hand once again over the sea, the ice walls begin melting, and the Egyptians try desperately to outrun the melt. They're not making it. Not even one of them (Ex. 14:23-28).

Scene four is not a pretty sight but shows us picture of *faith's preservation*. Hundreds of thousands of bodies are washing up on the shore of the Red Sea. Is it ugly? Yes it is. But this is what Israel saw, and this scene's sign reads, *"Israel saw that great work which the Lord did upon the Egyptians, and the people feared the Lord, and BELIEVED the Lord, and His servant Moses"* (Exodus 14:31). Now keep this in mind; these people struggled to see *faith's preservation* on the other side of the sea. These were the ones who were convinced God had brought them out here only because the cemeteries in Egypt were too small (Exodus 14:11). But they had a leader who not only could see this preservation but, by faith, demonstrated it by telling the sons of Israel to move forward.

Faith's preservation will manifest itself corporately when a leader of faith encourages the sons of God to move forward, *even* in the midst of a seemingly impossible situation. It will manifest when a leader of faith has the boldness to say, "Why are you crying out to God? Move forward! Press on toward the goal for the prize of the upward call of God in Christ Jesus!" When that leader stretches out his hand and releases the anointing of God in the midst of the enemy's trap, *faith's preservation* is manifested. We've seen it in Moses, Gideon, Esther and David. From Genesis to Revelation we see men and women, leaders of faith, stand up in the midst of dire circumstances, release the anointing, and deliver God's children through the manifestation of *faith's preservation*.

Will you be that man? Will you be that woman? Will you be a leader of enduring faith who will stand up, release God's anointing and deliver a child of God from bondage through *faith's preservation*?

Chapter 11

FAITH'S MIRACLE

Faith's Miracle

The tour takes us to exhibit #15 where "Faith's Miracle" is demonstrated in the lives of the Israelites. We have seen how *faith's preservation* was manifested in the deliverance of the Israelites from the Egyptian army right through the middle of the Red Sea. We have seen how a leader of faith can manifest this preservation by releasing the anointing and exhorting people to move forward. We are about to see another leader of faith, Joshua, move a nation to demonstrate *faith's miracle* for us. The entrance sign at this exhibit reads, *"By faith the walls of Jericho fell down after they had been encircled for seven days"* (Hebrews 11:30). As impressive as falling walls may be, I'm sure it does not start here. Let's see how this exhibit does begin.

In scene one, we find Joshua, near Jericho, face to face with a man who has his sword drawn. Listen. Joshua asks Him, *"Are you for us or for our adversaries?"* This man answers, *"No, rather I indeed come now as captain of the host of the Lord"* (Josh. 5:13-15). This is no man. This is God! This is the One who promised to go before Israel and lead them into Canaan. Recognizing Him, Joshua worships the One he thought was a man. He now recognizes Him as God, the Captain of Israel. He calls Him "Adon," meaning Sovereign, Lord, Master, Owner. He asks, *"What has my Lord to say to his servant?"* He recognizes himself as God's servant. *This* is the beginning of *faith's miracle*.

Recognizing God and yourself as God's servant is the beginning of *faith's miracle*. Without this recognition there will be no fallen walls. Look at the recognition. It comes without wind. It comes without rocks breaking. It comes without earthquake. It comes without fire. The recognition comes in a still small voice, the voice of a man. God, who looks like a man, stands like a man, and holds a sword like a man, speaks with an audible voice like a man, and like Elijah, Joshua hears the words of this still small voice and recognizes that it is God. The man does not define God. His physical appearance does not bring recognition, but His Words reveal who He is. The first step toward manifesting *faith's miracle* is hearing the WORDS of God's still small voice and recognizing that it is Him.

In scene two, God repeats to Joshua what He said to Moses, *"Remove your sandals from your feet, for this place where you are standing is holy"* (Josh. 6:15). Joshua recognizes that this dirt is now holy because of the Lord's presence. This is the second step in manifesting faith's miracle, recognizing holy ground. Until we recognize that this ground, this clay that we are walking around *in*, yes *in*, is holy because of the Lord's presence, we will not be able to manifest *faith's miracle*. As long as we insist on keeping our sandals of self-righteousness on, and walking around in our shoes of man's holiness, we will not depend on the arm of the Lord and faith's miracle will circumvent us. Joshua recognizes that this dirt outside the walls of Jericho is no different than the dirt anywhere else. But the Lord says it is holy, and for Joshua, that makes it holy.

Recognize that the dirt you are walking around *in* is no different than the dirt anyone else is walking around *in* except for the fact that God has declared *it* His temple, has made *it* His place of residence, and that His presence *alone* makes *it* holy ground!

We've recognized God by His words. We've recognized holy ground by His presence. Let's continue in this exhibit on our way to *faith's miracle*. In scene three we are at Jericho. The gates are closed. The city is tightly shut, no one coming or going. The people of Jericho know *who* is coming. Your enemy knows when you are on the way. He knows when you have recognized God, have heard His word, and have begun to see yourself as holy ground. He starts to batten down the hatches. He begins to entrench himself. He prepares to "hold his ground". He wants to discourage you. He wants you to look at the walls, the gates, the fortifications, and say, "No way! No way can I defeat this thing! No way will I be able to make a breakthrough!"

The enemy wants you to think that you must live with this fortified city in your life. But God has other plans. He tells Joshua about them. He says, "*See.*" The first instruction to Joshua is, "*See.*" We need to open our eyes. The first thing we need to do is "*see.*" The first thing. Not the last. Not after the walls are down.

Faith's miracle begins by "*seeing*". If you cannot see the walls flattened before they are, you cannot begin to carry out the instructions of *faith's miracle*! He goes on, "*See, I have given Jericho into your hand, with its king and the valiant warriors*" (Joshua 6:2).

Enduring faith walkers, can you see *your Jericho* given into your hand, along with its king, Satan, and his demonic forces? Can you see yourself in authority over him, treading upon him and over all his power? Or are you only able to see the enemy in authority over you, his walls standing, and his demonic warriors running rampant in your life? It *starts* with seeing. It starts with seeing the finished work of God's plan.

But there is more. God gives Joshua instruction on what he is to do. *"You shall march around the city, all the men of war circling the city once. Do so for six days, then on the seventh day march around the city seven times, and the priests shall blow the trumpets"* (Joshua 6:3-4). God gives Joshua the specifics. We have already addressed the importance of paying attention to the specifics in seeing the manifestations of faith. Let's see if Joshua pays attention.

Joshua goes. They take up the Ark of the Covenant. Seven priests are carrying seven trumpets of ram's horns, and along with the armed men they are going before it as they begin to march around the city. Joshua is doing it, just like God told him. They are blowing the trumpets, but look, all the rest are silent, mouths held tightly shut, just like Joshua commanded them, *"You shall not shout, nor let your voice be heard, nor let a word proceed out of your mouth"* (Josh 6:10).

Isn't this where we get messed up? We fail to pay attention to the specifics. But Joshua has been here before, forty years earlier. He was with a bunch of boys who couldn't keep their jaws from flapping about how it looked. He remembered what happened to those boys who spoke the "bad report" of what they saw. He spoke the good report then and he's not going to have any grasshopper stories now. These Israelites may have thoughts that they are grasshoppers to these walls, but they sure are not going to give voice to those thoughts on this march. Joshua commanded, *"Speak not a word!"* He understood.

But we fail to understand. We take up the ark. We grab our trumpets all right. We even begin to march around our Jerichos. But what we don't do is keep our mouths shut. We start blabbing to each other about how big our Jericho walls are. We double the height and triple the width. We exaggerate the fortifications. Oh, we keep marching, but continue to talk about how strong the walls are, how powerful the king and his men inside are, how impossible it will be for these walls to ever come down. Every day we go out and march around the city. But we continue to destroy our faith by seeing the walls standing, not fallen, and speaking them higher and stronger than they really are.

We have missed a major specific. We need to learn to shut our mouths and just blow the trumpet until its time to shout. If we keep our lips on the trumpet, our lips cannot tell grasshopper stories. The manifestation of *faith's miracle* will evade us until we put a guard over our mouth and a door (or a trumpet) on our lips (Psalm 141:3). The door is God's Word. Place His Word against your lips and blow. If we need something to blow about, we should blow about God's Word.

In scene four we find Joshua once again leading Israel in the specifics. This is the seventh day and they have now circled the city twelve times. This is the 13th march around Jericho, the last one God told them to take. Watch what unfolds. As they come to the end, Joshua gives the command, *"Shout! For the Lord has given you the city!"* But that's not all; he goes on, *"The city shall be under the ban, it and all that is in it belongs to the Lord! Keep yourselves from things under the ban, lest you covet them and take some bringing trouble to the camp"* (Josh. 6:16-18).

Here again we see our downfall. The Lord gives Jerichos into our hands, but we covet the things within the walls of our Jerichos. We covet them until we take them and bring trouble into our camps again. We are grateful for the freedom but want to hang on to the things that brought the walls into existence in the first place.

We shout and thank the Lord that our Jericho walls have fallen, that the enemy king is no longer entrenched in our lives, and yet we continue to entertain the very thoughts that built those Jericho walls and entrenched the enemy king. It's like we start all over, hoping that our covetousness will not lead to a Jericho again, or that if it does then God will once again deliver those Jericho walls into our hands. And He will (Psalm 107:6, 13, 19-20, 28-30). He will deliver us over and over again. But why do we act like the Israelites on a roller coaster ride through the desert? Give the spoils of your Jericho victories into the treasury of the Lord. The spoils from our Jericho victories belong to the Lord.

All the passions and lusts, the wants and desires, the plea-sures and things that built your Jericho walls, when placed in the treasury of the Lord are returned to you in their appropriate design. He wants you to have passion, but it belongs to Him. He wants you to lust, but only after Him. Wants and desires? His way is to give us His (Psalm 37:4). What about pleasures and things? He is *for* these, but He wants them to flow from Him, from the seeking of His kingdom (Matthew 6:33). All these "things" we covet belong to Him. They are holy to the Lord (Josh 6:19). He wants to give them to us, but in their rightful state. We cannot gain them for ourselves and receive them in their rightful state, for apart from Him they are all perverted. That is why they belong to Him, not out of God's self-ishness, but out of God's *perfect* generosity. This is an important paradox: they belong to Him out of His perfect generosity.

Listen as the priests blow the trumpets. The people shout with a great shout! Look at those walls. Falling down flat. So flat that the Israelites run right into the city and overtake it, the result of foolishness. Obedient foolishness. Foolishly marching in silence around a city blowing trumpets. No efforts to scale the walls. No weapons or engines of siege only a merry-making spectacle to the Jerichonians. But God, who takes the foolish things and confounds the wise, pushed those walls right down into the earth enabling the Israeli men of war to rush in and take the city.

This foolishness is our weapon of warfare too. It is idiotic to the senses, for it is not of the senses, but of the divine. It is of divine power for the purpose of destroying our fortresses. It is not according to our plans. It is not rational, and it does not fit into our methodology. It is a spiritual machine, a super war machine, like a spiritual Apache combat helicopter that targets and destroys spec-ulations. It targets and annihilates imaginations that are contrary to God's knowledge. It spots enemy thoughts, drops in, handcuffs them, and takes them into captivity, captivity to the obedience of Christ (2 Cor. 10:4). With this weapon we deliver outlaw thoughts to Christ saying, "Jesus, here is an outlaw thought. I've cuffed him for You. Take him into custody!"

Thoughts held captive to the obedience of Christ are what we see in this exhibit manifesting *faith's miracle.* They are utterly destroying everything in the city with the edge of the sword, burning it and destroying the perversion. But the silver, the gold, the bronze and iron, they are bringing out to put in the treasury of the Lord. Do you understand? Imaginations are good when captivated by God. Speculations are grand when they are according to the knowledge of God. And thoughts are powerful when they are in line with the mind of Christ.

There is more to *faith's miracle* than just marching around your Jericho. There are instructions. There are specifics. Joshua paid attention to the specifics, saw the manifestation of *faith's miracle*, and Joshua 6:27 says, *"So the Lord was with Joshua, and his fame was in all the land."* What does enduring faith do? Enduring faith pays attention to the specifics and manifests *faith's miracle!*

But someone messed it up for the sons of Israel. A man by the name of Achan acted unfaithfully and thirty-six Israeli soldiers lost their lives in what should have been a no-contest battle. The great walls of Jericho came down for the Israelites, but because of covetousness, the victors of Jericho became the victims of Ai. You don't want to experience an Ai so...

Manifest Faith's Miracle by:

1. Recognizing God, hearing the still small voice of His word.
2. Recognizing holy ground. Taking off your sandals of self-righteousness, your shoes of man's holiness and magnifying His presence in residence.
3. Beginning to "see" your Jericho walls fallen. You've got to look into the spiritual realm and "see" what God is doing.
4. Keeping your mouth shut about how big the walls appear. This goes against the senses. Something in us wants to let others know the size of our battle, how big what we are up against is.

5. Making a decision to not covet anything, good or bad, within the walls of Jericho.

6. Foolishly shouting when the Lord tells you to shout. Do it His way, no matter how ridiculous it seems. Lay aside the logical, the rational, and pick up the *spiritual* weapon of war.

Then watch the fortresses be destroyed by "faith's miracle" – a Divine Strategy of spiritual warfare for taking out the Jerichos in your life!

Chapter 12

FAITH'S DELIVERANCE

Faith's Deliverance

In exhibit #16 "Faith's Deliverance" is manifested through the faith of Rahab. This is a large exhibit. The Master Architect has much for us to experience in *faith's deliverance*.

The opening scene is described by this sign, *"Then Joshua the son of Nun sent two men as spies secretly from Shittim, saying, 'Go, view the land, especially Jericho.' So they went and came into the house of a harlot whose name was Rahab, and lodged there"*– Joshua 2:1 *"By faith Rahab the harlot did not perish along with those who were disobedient, after she had welcomed the spies in peace"* (Hebrews 11:31).

Exhibit #16 opens with Joshua *secretly* sending out two spies, and only two, to view the land, even Jericho. God shows us something we should learn from the past. In our last exhibit we saw how Joshua commanded the men of war not to speak a word as they marched around the walls of Jericho. We understood this to be a result of the lessons learned at Kadesh-barnea 40 years earlier where the Israelites defied God.

Scene two of exhibit #16 takes us back those 40 years to the events so influential in Joshua's life that it changed his faith walk forever. The Lord would have us revisit the events surrounding the defiance of His Word before we continue to explore *faith's deliverance*. These events are interconnected.

Scene two begins as Moses declares to Israel the intentions God had for them to take possession of the Promised Land. *"The LORD our God spoke to us at Horeb, saying, 'You have stayed long enough at this mountain. See, I have placed the land before you; go in and possess the land which the LORD swore to give to your fathers, to Abraham, to Isaac, and to Jacob, to them and their descendants after them.' Then we set out from Horeb, and went through all that great and terrible wilderness which you saw on the way to the hill country of the Amorites, just as the LORD our God had commanded us; and we came to Kadesh-barnea. I said to you, 'You have come to the hill country of the Amorites which the LORD our God is about to give us. See, the LORD your God has placed the land before you; go up, take possession, as the LORD, the God of your fathers, has spoken to you. Do not fear or be dismayed.' Then all of you approached me and said, 'Let us send men before us, that they may search out the land for us, and bring back to us word of the way by which we should go up and the cities which we shall enter'"* (Deut. 1:6, 8, 19-22).

Moses tells the Israelites that God had wanted them to go in and take possession of the Promised Land, but instead they had approached Moses saying, "Let us send *men* before we go so that they might spy it out and tell us how we can take the land." Here is our first lesson; they are choosing the wrong source for a *"word of the way"*. The Israelites are looking in the wrong direction. They are looking at themselves, instead of up at the cloud that has gone before them. Moses reprimands them for this, *"You are not willing to go up, but are rebelling against the command of the LORD your God"* (Deut. 1:26). He tries to convince them the Lord Himself will fight on their behalf, just as He'd done in Egypt (Deut. 1:30-31).

"Israel, what is wrong with the cloud of the Lord's glory that led you across the wilderness in the day? Is it no longer good enough to take you into the land of promise? And what of the Pillar of His fire that shines by night? Is it no longer bright enough for you to trust God to show you the way in? You do not trust the Lord your God!" Moses continues, *"But for all this, you did not trust the LORD your God, who goes before you on your way, to seek out a place for you to encamp, in fire by night and cloud by day, to show you the way in which you should go"* (Deut. 1:32-33).

God wants the Israelites to simply go in and take possession of their land, which He intends to hand over, and they are begging to send men in on a spy mission. They are looking in the wrong direction and to the wrong source. Nevertheless, in scene three we hear the Lord giving Moses, along with His promise, permission and instructions to spy out the land of Canaan. *"Send out for yourself men so that they may spy out the land of Canaan, which I am going to give to the sons of Israel; you shall send a man from each of their fathers' tribes, every one a leader among them"* (Numbers 13:2). This is God's Word to them, *"...land, which I am going to give to Israel."* This is truth. God spoke it (Jn. 17:17).

Moses selects leaders from each tribe. He instructs them to spy out the land of Canaan saying, *"Go up there into the Negev; then go up into the hill country. See what the land is like, and whether the people who live in it are strong or weak, whether they* are few or many. How is the land in which they live, is it good or bad? And how are the cities in which they live, are they like open camps or with fortifications? How is the land, is it fat or lean? Are there trees in it or not? Make an effort then to get some of the fruit of the land"* (Numbers 13:17-20). Moses sends these 12 spies out to bring back a report of the land. The sign under this scene reads, *"So they went up and spied out the land from the wilderness of Zin as far as Rehob, at Lebo-hamath. Then they came to the valley of Eshcol and from there cut down a branch with a single cluster of grapes; and they carried it on a pole between two men, with some of the pomegranates and the figs"* (Numbers 13:21-23).

Scene four opens with their return, *"When they returned from spying out the land, at the end of forty days..."* **(Numbers 13:25).** Forty days they spent on this mission. Israel will soon wish it had only been one. The spies returned to Kadesh, bringing to Israel the word of *man* that they had requested and showing them the fruit. Listen to what they say. *"We went in to the land where you sent us; and it certainly does flow with milk and honey, and this is its fruit. Nevertheless..."* – Nevertheless? Nevertheless? Moses never asked for a nevertheless! What is this nevertheless stuff? *"Nevertheless, the people who live in the land are strong, and the cities are fortified and very large; and moreover, we saw the descendants of Anak there. Amalek is living in the land of the Negev and the Hittites and the Jebusites and the Amorites are living in the hill country, and the Canaanites are living by the sea and by the side of the Jordan"* (Numbers 13:27-29).

The people murmur. Caleb interrupts this *nevertheless* and quiets the people, *"We should by all means go up and take posses-sion of it, for we will surely overcome it"* (Numbers 13:30). Caleb

102

has grabbed hold of the truth. He understands that what God says is a greater reality. He said, "By all means we should go up, for we shall surely overcome!"

That sounds like the words coming out of that exhibit entitled "Faith's Authority," doesn't it? Turn your ears toward the hall. Do you hear Joseph? *"God will surely take care of you! You shall surely carry my bones into the Promised Land!"* Certainly Caleb hears this and speaks with the same authority. Certainly Caleb hears these faith words echoing through time and speaks them into the present with the same authority of faith with which Joseph first spoke them. Perhaps Caleb was even one who was commissioned to carry Joseph's bones.

But the other spies will have nothing to do with truth, *"We are not able to go up against the people, for they are too strong for us"* (Num. 13:31). Sadly they missed the purpose of the mission. Moses didn't send them out there to evaluate the Israelite's ability. He didn't ask them to make a military invasion decision. But what should we expect when we send out a man to do a Creator's job? This is lesson number two: Never send a man to do a Creator's job.

What should we expect when we get our assessment from man, and not the One who created him? We should expect exactly what these Israelites got, an evil report. The sign tells us, *"So they gave out to the sons of Israel a bad report of the land which they had spied out"* (Numbers 13:32). The other spies speak, *"The land through which we have gone, in spying it out, is a land that devours its inhabitants; and all the people whom we saw in it are men of great size. There also we saw the Nephilim; and we became like grasshoppers in our own sight, and so we were in their sight"* (Numbers 13:32-33). In our own sight...therein lies the problem with sending men to assess the situation. They look at it *in their own sight*, and then speculate how it looks *in the sight of others*. They then advise you to move based on their vision, or the lack thereof, and what they perceive to be the vision of friend and foe.

These were the grasshopper stories that Joshua would not allow to be repeated during the march around Jericho. Grasshopper stories are faith killers. You might say, "Well, they were just speaking the facts." That is correct, but what God wanted them to do was speak the truth. He called the facts an evil report because truth prevails over facts and He wanted the truth spoken so it could prevail. Facts are derived from sense knowledge, but truth is gained through spirit knowledge, revelation knowledge of the spirit realm. God wanted the truth spoken so it could prevail. In this situation God's *will* did not prevail because facts were reported instead of truth. Sense realm knowledge reigned while spirit realm knowledge was suppressed. God's *will* did not prevail because sense realm knowledge (facts) reigned instead of spirit realm knowledge (truth). Facts were spoken and given the preeminence over truth, thus giving facts the upper hand.

The people of Israel give credence to this evil report. The entire congregation lifts up their voices, crying, weeping, and grumbling (Num. 14:1). They rail against Moses and Aaron saying, *"Would that we had died in the land of Egypt! Or would that we had died in this wilderness"* (Num. 14:2)! They're going to regret that one, along with that forty-day spy mission. But they just won't shut-up. Listen. *"Why is the LORD bringing us into this land, to fall by the sword? Our wives and our little ones will become plunder; would it not be better for us to return to Egypt? Let us appoint a leader and return to Egypt"* (Numbers 14:3-4). Why this desire to return to slavery? All because they heard and believed man's report, a bad report.

They consider the facts. But what do facts generate? Unbelief. They do not believe God's Word. The Word that said, *"I have given you the land,"* must mean *nothing* to them. But look! The leaders, Moses and Aaron, fall on their faces in front of the people. God desires that leaders today respond in like manner when faced with complaint, insubordination, and insurrection.

Joshua, our Jericho man, comes onto the scene with Caleb. They're tearing their clothes and addressing the people. Listen. *"The land which we passed through to spy out is an exceedingly good land. If the LORD is pleased with us, then He will bring us into this land and give it to us— a land which flows with milk and honey. Only do not rebel against the LORD; and do not fear the people of the land, for they will be our prey. Their protection has been removed from them, and the LORD is with us; do not fear them"* (Num. 14:7-9).

Finally, someone stands up and speaks truth. This is the good report, the one God wants spoken. Joshua and Caleb are not considering the facts like the other ten spies; they are only considering the truth of what God said, causing them to speak the "good report". It is good and refreshing when someone speaks the truth over facts. Surely this is what motivates people to rise up and reach the potential God has ascribed to them. Let's see if this moves the Israelites to faith and gets them excited about what God is doing for them.

But, no, they're picking up stones. They want to stone Joshua and Caleb. Why? Why wouldn't people want to hear the truth? Why would anyone want to destroy someone who brings great news of victory? Why would people want to believe the evil report over the good one? I don't understand. But it looks like the deliberations are over, and they're over now, for the glory of the Lord is appearing in the tent of meeting! The Lord is speaking to Moses, *"How long will this people spurn Me? And how long will they not believe in Me, despite all the signs which I have performed in their midst? I will smite them with pestilence and dispossess them, and I will make you into a nation greater and mightier than they"* (Num. 14:11-12). No, no, no! Is this what comes of the evil report?

Wait; Moses tries to talk God out of it. Oh, Moses *is* persuasive! "God, if you destroy them, people will say you couldn't deliver them." Good argument Moses. Man, you're bold. Listen, God responds to Moses, *"I have pardoned them according to your word"* (Num. 14:20). Wow! Apparently God likes boldness! That must be why He wants *us* to approach His throne in boldness and with confidence. He responds to confidence. He responds to boldness.

This wasn't the first time Moses applied boldness. We've seen it all along in God's faith men and women; Abraham, Jacob, Gideon, David, and Elijah. We've seen it in the centurion, the woman with the issue of blood, the Syrophonecian woman, and Jairus. All the great ones of faith come with absolute confidence and boldness in their Father, their Lord, and their Master. We never see them come in ducking, and bowing, and scraping. And God always calls it "great faith". He wants people who believe, who really believe in Him. But listen, He goes on, *"but indeed, as I live, all the earth will be filled with the glory of the LORD. Surely all the men who have seen My glory and My signs which I performed in Egypt and in the wilderness, yet have put Me to the test these ten times and have not listened to My voice, shall by no means see the land which I swore to their fathers, nor shall any of those who spurned Me see it"* (Numbers 14:21-23).

Makes you want to listen to His voice, the good report, the truth. Apparently if you consider the facts and allow them to supercede the truth, you will not see the land, you will not see the promise. This is one of the foundations for seeing *faith's deliverance*. Listen, God talks about Caleb now, *"But My servant Caleb, because he has had a different spirit and has followed Me fully, I will bring into the land which he entered, and his descendants shall take possession of it"* (Numbers 14:24). Caleb gets to go in! Speaking the good report got him results. Speaking the good report means you're walking in the promise. I wonder when he'll get to go in. Maybe tomorrow.

Oh, God's talking again, this time to Moses and Aaron, *"How long shall I bear with this evil congregation who are grumbling against Me? I have heard the complaints of the sons of Israel, which they are making against Me. Say to them, 'As I live,' says the LORD, 'just as you have spoken in My hearing, so I will surely do to you'"* (Numbers 14:27-28). What was it they spoke? Oh yeah, *"Would that we had died in the land of Egypt! Or would that we had died in this wilderness"* (Num. 14:2)! This doesn't look good. God continues to speak, *"your corpses will fall in this wilderness, even all your numbered men, according to your complete number from twenty years old and upward, who have grumbled against Me"* (Numbers 14:29). So this is where *what you say is what you get* comes from. Oh, the dangers of speaking the evil report.

Jesus always asked, *"What do you want?"* and then said *"Be it done unto you according to your faith."* What He must have meant was "according to what you spoke in faith." These Israelites spoke the bad report in faith and God says, "Be it done unto you according to your faith." I don't know about you, but get me Psalm 141:3, and get it to me quick. *"Set a guard Oh Lord, over my mouth; keep watch over the door of my lips!"*

God continues, *"Surely you shall not come into the land in which I swore to settle you, except Caleb the son of Jephunneh and Joshua the son of Nun."* (Numbers 14:30) Both Joshua and Caleb, those "good reporters", get to go in. Maybe it will be soon. *"Your children, however, whom you said would become a prey—I will bring them in, and they will know the land which you have rejected. But as for you, your corpses will fall in this wilderness. Your sons shall be shepherds for forty years in the wilderness, and they will suffer for your unfaithfulness, until your corpses lie in the wilderness. According to the number of days which you spied out the land, forty days, for every day you shall bear your guilt a year, even forty years, and you will know My opposition. I, the LORD, have spoken, surely this I will do to all this evil congregation who are gathered together against Me. In this wilderness they shall be destroyed, and there they will die"* (Numbers 14:31-35).

Soon isn't tomorrow. Forty years? Isn't that a long time to stand in faith? Why do they need to suffer for the others unfaithfulness? Is it possible that I suffer because of others unfaithfulness? Is it possible that *others* suffer because of *my* unfaithfulness? Is it possible that there are Joshuas and Calebs out there in the wilderness because of my unfaithfulness? Forty years? So long! Is it worth it?

Look! The ten spies who returned with the bad report and made the people grumble against God are dying. A plague has hit them, but Joshua and Caleb remain standing. God says it is because of the *very bad* report that they brought out (Numbers

14:36-37). He calls their report of the Promised Land a very bad report. All they did was state the facts. God doesn't want us living by facts, but by faith, even if it's for forty years. Looking at this answers my question, "Is it worth it?" The alternative isn't pretty. Preacher, give me that good report; I only want to consider the truth. "Lord, it is my desire to never cause anyone to grumble by speaking the bad report!"

The Israelites are getting the message. They are all in mourning. Listen to them wail. They are truly sorry. Such repentance will surely move the heart of God. Look at them now, though. They are heading up to the ridge of the hill country. Listen to what they're saying? *"Here we are; we have sinned, but we will go up to the place where the Lord has promised"* (Numbers 14:40).

This sounds like us. We speak the bad report, we talk negatively, and then when harvest time comes we want to reap the promise. Why not? I'm always sorry for not believing. Besides, I want to reap.

Here comes Moses. Listen to what he says, *"Why then are you transgressing the commandment of the LORD, when it will not succeed? Do not go up, or you will be struck down before your enemies, for the LORD is not among you. For the Amalekites and the Canaanites will be there in front of you, and you will fall by the sword, inasmuch as you have turned back from following the LORD. And the LORD will not be with you"* (Numbers 14:41-43).

I can hear God saying to me, *"Do not be deceived, God is not mocked; for whatever a man sows, this he will also reap"* (Gal. 6:7). But I want a harvest. I want a harvest. I'm going for it. I'm going to get my promise. I know I haven't sown the right seeds, but I'm going to act on the promise now.

The Israelites are going on up. They heedlessly head up to the ridge of the hill country with no Ark of the Covenant of the Lord and no Moses. Are they crazy? What is wrong with them, trying to reap a harvest without sowing? They should know better. They didn't believe when they were supposed to believe. They can't go in now. Moses told them, "No!"

They're getting slaughtered. The Amelekites and Canaanites are beating them down! What were they thinking? They were thinking the same thing I've been thinking. That I can sow a field full of negative seed, that I can meditate on and speak the facts, the bad report, and then somehow, come harvest time, reap the truth. But it doesn't work like that. God is not mocked. I will reap what I sow! Why do we try to operate this way, and then blame God when we get mowed down? Why, when we are on our *own,* reaping in our *own* fields, which we have sown *ourselves,* do we grumble to *God* about the harvest?

I'm sure these events in scene 4 of Exhibit #16 are embedded in Joshua's mind. Continue on to scene 5 and see how this has influenced Joshua in his faith walk in the exhibit demonstrating *faith's deliverance.*

In scene 5, the two Israeli spies depart having been secretly sent by their commander Joshua. Joshua has learned that a public spy mission would only enhance the opportunity for panic in the camp should the spies return with a bad report like his ten counterparts forty years earlier. He has sworn them to secrecy. He has also learned that sending only two increases the odds in his favor of receiving a good report. If only one comes back with a good report, Joshua will be able to stand with him against the third in a two to one ruling.

They head off to Jericho where the gates of the city are still open. They seek lodging at the house of the harlot, Rahab. This should be interesting. What are they thinking? How can you trust someone like that? Uh, oh! It looks like the game is up. The king's men just showed up. They grab Rahab and shout at her, *"Bring out the men who have come to you, who have entered your house, for they have come to search out all the land"* (Josh. 2:3). These two spies picked the wrong place to find lodging. Rahab is going to turn them in. No, wait! She responds, *"Yes, the men came to me, but I did not know where they were from. It came about when it was time to shut the gate at dark that the men went out; I do not know where the men went. Pursue them quickly, for you will over- take them"* (Josh. 2:4-5).

This is unexpected. As the king's men leave, she goes back in her house, built right on the city wall. The king's men head out on the Jordan road as the gates to the city shut behind them. The spies will be trapped when those men come back from their wild goose chase.

Rahab is on her roof now. She moves some stalks of flax. The two spies emerge from where she had hidden them on her roof. She talks to them. Listen to her faith, *"I know that the LORD has given you the land, and that the terror of you has fallen on us, and that all the inhabitants of the land have melted away before you. For we have heard how the LORD dried up the water of the Red Sea before you when you came out of Egypt, and what you did to the two kings of the Amorites who were beyond the Jordan, to Sihon and Og, whom you utterly destroyed. When we heard it, our hearts melted and no courage remained in any man any longer because of you; for the LORD your God, He is God in heaven above and on earth beneath. Now therefore, please swear to me by the LORD, since I have dealt kindly with you, that you also will deal kindly with my father's household, and give me a pledge of truth, and spare my father and my mother and my brothers and my sisters, with all who belong to them, and deliver our lives from death"* (Josh. 2:9-13).

This Jericho woman is not only intelligent but has faith in the God of Israel. She foresees the destruction of her city and is planning for the salvation of her family. How will these spies from Israel respond? They lay out a contract for her, *"Our life for yours if you do not tell this business of ours; and it shall come about when the LORD gives us the land that we will deal kindly and faithfully with you"* (Josh. 2:14). She agrees to it.

She leads them over to a window in the wall where she throws a cord out the window and ties it off to a beam. She plans their escape, *"Go to the hill country, so that the pursuers will not happen upon you, and hide yourselves there for three days until the pursuers return. Then afterward you may go on your way"* (Josh. 2:16). Rahab is a very intelligent woman of faith!

The spies, at the window and ready to escape, speak to Rahab, *"We shall be free from this oath to you which you have made us swear, unless, when we come into the land, you tie this cord of scarlet thread in the window through which you let us down, and gather to yourself into the house your father and your mother and your brothers and all your father's household. It shall come about that anyone who goes out of the doors of your house into the street, his blood shall be on his own head, and we shall be free; but anyone who is with you in the house, his blood shall be on our head if a hand is laid on him. But if you tell this business of*

ours, then we shall be free from the oath which you have made
us swear" (Josh. 2:17-20).

They have laid out the details of the contract. She is going
to have to step out and share her faith with family members, tell
them this outrageous story of salvation, and invite them into her
home on the day of battle. She will have to trust that a small scarlet
thread hanging in her window will keep the walls supporting her
house standing and her family alive. Rahab will have to put action
behind her faith. This must be what James meant when he said,
"*In the same way, was not Rahab the harlot also justified by works
when she received the messengers and sent them out by another
way*" (James 2:25)? Rahab answers, "*According to your words,
so be it*" (Josh. 2:21). She is going to do it. She sends them away
and ties the scarlet cord in the window.

The two spies, upon returning to the Israeli camp, talk to Joshua.
They emulate Joshua and Caleb forty years before. "*Surely the
LORD has given all the land into our hands; moreover, all the
inhabitants of the land have melted away before us*" (Josh. 2:24).
They have chosen and spoken the good report. Joshua must have
selected two men of faith who would choose to view God's Word
as their reality over the overwhelming sight of Jericho's walls.
Good move Joshua, you learned well.

Scene six looks very familiar. The Israeli trumpets blow. The
walls of Jericho compress right into the ground. All of the walls are
obliterated except for the section Rahab's house stands on. There
is her window, the scarlet thread blows in the wind. She has followed her contract to the letter.

Joshua speaks to the messengers he sent to spy out Jericho,
"*Go into the harlot's house and bring the woman and all she has*

out of there, as you have sworn to her" (Josh.6:22). The messengers climb the stairs on this narrow section of remaining Jericho wall. They bring out Rahab, and her father, and her mother, and her brother, and all her relatives and all her possessions. They take them to the camp of Israel. Joshua and his men burn Jericho. Rahab and her actions of faith save her family and herself from destruction.

Faith's deliverance manifested through faith in a thin scarlet cord! *This* is what took Rahab to Faith's Hall of Fame to be "headlined" over Joshua, her deliverer. This is what placed this harlot's name in the genealogy of Jesus Christ with four other women of faith mentioned in Matthew chapter one. The Master Architect would have us understand that He does not measure how *big* our faith exploits are, but how *pure* our trust in His Word is. It is not how *dutifully* we live our lives, but how *beautifully* we respond in faith.

Of the five women mentioned in Christ's genealogy, three had lived tainted lives. Tamar and Bathsheba were adulteresses, and Rahab a harlot. Only Ruth and Mary were "pure" women, and some would question Ruth's behavior on the night she slept at Boaz's feet (Ruth 3:7-14). Many of Faith's Hall of Fame "headliners" failed miserably at one time or another during their faith journey. *Faith's deliverance* is not dependent on an upright life but an upright faith.

Chapter 13

FAITH'S MIRACULOUS VICTORY

Faith's Miraculous Victory

The plaque on exhibit #17 informs us Gideon is demonstrating "Faith's Miraculous Victory" for us. The Israelites live in caves and dens hiding from the Midianites. The Midianites destroy the Israelite's crops. They devastate Israel's land, rob them of new crops, take their sheep, oxen, and donkeys. The Israelis cry out to the Lord. God hears their cry. He sends a prophet to speak to them. *"Thus says the LORD, the God of Israel, It was I who brought you up from Egypt and brought you out from the house of slavery. I delivered you from the hands of the Egyptians and from the hands of all your oppressors, and dispossessed them before you and gave you their land, and I said to you, 'I am the LORD your God; you shall not fear the gods of the Amorites in whose land you live. But you have not obeyed Me'"* (Judges 6:8-10). This is the reason for the seven years of servitude to the Midianites (Judges 6:1). But faith's miraculous victory must be about to bring it to an end.

In scene two Gideon beats wheat in that wine press. He figures it would be the last place the Midianites would suspect to find goods to pilfer since the vineyards have been stripped. But someone knows he's in there flailing wheat. A man enters. It's the Lord Himself. He speaks, *"The LORD is with you, O valiant warrior"* (Judges 6:12). This Gideon fellow sure does not look like a valiant warrior. He doesn't sound like one either. *"O my lord, if the LORD is with us, why then has all this happened to us? And where are all His miracles which our fathers told us about, saying, 'Did not the LORD bring us up from Egypt?' But now the LORD has abandoned us and given us into the hand of Midian"* (Judges 6:13). This guy is in the faith hall? He sounds more like a complaining loser.

But the Lord looks at Gideon, shakes His head and says, *"Go in this your strength and deliver Israel from the hand of Midian. Have I not sent you"* (Judges 6:14)? What is God calling Gideon's strength? God's Word. God's Word to him, *"The Lord is with you, O valiant warrior,"* is the strength Gideon is to use to deliver Israel. This must be exactly the way it works for us, too. Our strength is in what God calls us in His Word. Our strength is not defined by the position we find ourselves in because of our circumstances. It is defined by how God views us.

But Gideon doesn't understand yet. *"O Lord, how shall I deliver Israel? Behold, my family is the least in Manasseh, and I am the youngest in my father's house"* (Judges 6:15). He still sees himself as a loser, the runt of the litter from a litter of losers. It may be easier for the Lord to work with this attitude than the opposite. There is no arrogance here, no self-righteousness, only the possibility of refuge in the name of the Lord God (Zeph. 3:11-12). It looks like God is going to work with him.

"Surely I will be with you, and you shall defeat Midian as one man" (Judges 6:16), God says to Gideon. Either Gideon is going to do it alone or the ones with him will be of one mind in this endeavor.

How will he respond? Gideon asks for a sign. God's Word is not good enough for him. Gideon asks God to stay put, as a sign to him, until he returns with an offering for Him. God agrees (Judges 6:17-18).

In scene three Gideon returns with a meal for the Lord and presents it to Him. God responds, *"Take the meat and the unleavened bread and lay them on this rock, and pour out the broth"* (Judges 6:20). Gideon soaks the bread and meat with the broth. What is going on? The Lord reaches out with His staff, touches the meat and the bread. Fire springs up from the rock and consumes the broth soaked meal! Certainly Gideon knows now that God is with him and will do through him what He said.

But no, this sign was not enough for Gideon. He asks God for another sign. He wants to place a fleece of wool on the threshing floor and tells God if it is wet with dew in the morning and the ground is dry then he will know that he is the one to deliver Israel. God agrees to it.

The next morning, in scene four, the fleece is as Gideon requested. He squeezes a whole bowl full of water from it. But he still asks for another sign. God surely missed it on this one. Gideon is no mighty warrior. How did this stonewalling wimp ever make it to the Faith Hall of Fame? Now he wants the fleece to be dry while the ground is wet.

We're never like this, are we? Well, there was that time when I... and times when I stonewalled when I knew God was telling me to proceed. Maybe we are more like Gideon than we'd like to admit. But God, in mercy, once again agrees to Gideon's request.

Gideon, in scene five, has his third sign confirmed. Is it enough? It must be, for he now gathers troops. Look at them come. There must be thousands. God speaks to Gideon telling him that the 32,000 are too many. He is afraid that Israel will become boastful, thinking it was their own power that delivered them.

God tells Gideon that all soldiers who are afraid can go home. All but 10,000 go. Gideon was afraid when God called on him too. What disqualified these 22,000 soldiers? "The same thing that disqualifies you; your unwillingness to remain." God says. *It is not your fear that disqualifies you, but your unwillingness to remain.* Gideon was afraid, but he was qualified because he was willing to *do it afraid*! That must be what took him to the " faith hall".

In scene six God talks to Gideon again, *"The people are still too many, Gideon!"* You've got to be kidding. There are 135,000 Midianites out there and God thinks 10,000 Israeli soldiers are too many? Since this exhibit is *faith's miraculous victory,* it might as well be big. God gives Gideon instructions for a test to whittle down his army. He is to take them to the water to drink and all who kneel to drink will be disqualified. As they go to the water, almost all of them kneel to drink. Gideon sends them home. He is left with only 300 soldiers now. They are now outnumbered 450 to 1! This *will* have to be a miraculous victory of faith for Gideon.

In scene seven Gideon arms his men. What is this? This army's weapons are trumpets and clay pitchers. These men are going to war with musical instruments and kitchen utensils. As they approach the Midianite camp, they spread out, encircling the camp. Then they stop and break the pitchers. Torches, previously hidden in each pitcher, flame brightly in the open air. The men blow the trumpets and hold the torches in the air. But they are not moving! The Midianites and their allies turn their swords on each other. They take each other out, while Gideon's army of 300 men simply stand in place around the camp armed with nothing but common household items!

We have a *Torch* burning on the inside of this jar of clay we live in (2 Cor. 4:7). It has been described as *"molten gold confined in the common cauldron of humanity"* (Thoene, *Jerusalem Gold*). The question we need to answer is how do we "break" the jar. How do we smash the pitcher? I wonder if blowing the trumpet of God's vision in us initiates the destruction. I wonder if brokenness begins occurring when, like Gideon, we are stripped of the use of our own resources. This appears to be God's paradox of resourcefulness; taking a man to where he depends on nothing and then using what that man has. I wonder if we will ever experience *Faith's Miraculous Victory* until we are willing to *do it afraid*.

I would guess Abraham was afraid when he left Ur of the Chaldeans. I bet Joseph was afraid when he was sent to prison. We know Moses was afraid when asked to deliver a nation. Samuel surely cried a few nights after his mother dropped him off with Eli. David must have shaken a little when, as a boy, he was anointed to be king over Israel. Esther was afraid to die approaching the king uninvited on behalf of her people. I'm sure Noah quaked for a moment here and there while building a boat to save mankind from extinction. What about Ruth when asked to make a move on Boaz? It wasn't the 21st century. And Jonah? We know where his fear took him. But every one of these men and women moved forward and decided to *do it afraid*.

What does enduring faith do? Enduring faith *does it afraid*! *Faith's Miraculous Victory* is accomplished only by the breaking of the pitcher, letting the torch burn, moving forward, and doing it afraid!

Chapter 14

FAITH'S TRIUMPH

Faith's Triumph

In exhibit #18 Barak demonstrates *Faith's Triumph* for us. But he shares this exhibit's marquee with two women. His triumph was delivered to him through the hands of these two women.

In the opening scene we find one of the women, Deborah, sitting under the palm tree of Deborah handing out rulings. She is the sitting judge over Israel and the sons of Israel are coming to her with their judicial issues. She sends out a summons to Barak. As he approaches, she speaks to him, *"Behold, the LORD, the God of Israel, has commanded, 'Go and march to Mount Tabor, and take with you ten thousand men from the sons of Naphtali and from the sons of Zebulun. I will draw out to you Sisera, the commander of Jabin's army, with his chariots and his many troops to the river Kishon, and I will give him into your hand'"* (Judges 4:6-7).

Barak is the man who will deliver Israel from twenty years of Canaanite oppression. This is going to be quite a feat, for Jabin's army has 900 iron chariots. Barak responds, *"If you will go with me, then I will go; but if you will not go with me, I will not go"* (Judges

4:8). Barak gives an ultimatum to the judge. He is not willing to receive the Word of the Lord as it is from her. Barak looks like the man in our last exhibit, a wimp who somehow makes it to the "Hall" in spite of his fear.

Deborah responds to his wimpy stonewalling, *"I will surely go with you; nevertheless, the honor shall not be yours on the journey that you are about to take, for the LORD will sell Sisera into the hands of a woman"* (Judges 4:9). This must be the reason for the shared marquee. Barak's fear creates the vacuum for two women warriors to rise to the occasion.

In scene two Deborah departs with Barak. Ten thousand men join up with this army led by Barak and Deborah. Deborah speaks again, *"Arise! For this is the day in which the LORD has given Sisera into your hands; behold, the LORD has gone out before you"* (Judges 4:14). After listening to this woman leading his army, Barak goes down from the mountain with his men following.

What are these spear-less, shield-less, unarmed men going to do against 900 iron chariots in the Midianite army? Where do they get the kind of faith to enter war in this way? As they charge against Sisera and his army, it starts to rain. No, it pours. Massively. The Kishon River is filling up, even flooding. The Midianite chariots are getting bogged down. Some are swept away.

A footnote was added to the exhibit some 1700 years later. "Napoleon defeated the Turks at this location in 1799 during a similar occurrence of flooding."

The Israeli soldiers pick up the Midianite's weapons and strike down the fleeing soldiers. This is an incredible triumph for an unarmed group of faith filled soldiers.

But Sisera escapes and heads off to Kedish where the Kenite, Heber has his tents pitched. He approaches the tent of Jael, Heber's wife. She comes out and speaks to him. *"Turn aside, my master, turn aside to me! Do not be afraid."* He goes into her tent. This is highly improper. According to Eastern custom this warrants the death penalty. This must be what Deborah meant when she told Barak that Sisera would be sold into the hands of a woman!

Scene three finds us inside Jael's tent. Jael covers Sisera with a rug. He asks for water. She opens a bottle of milk and he drinks from it. He asks her to deny he is there if anyone comes and asks. He goes to sleep, entirely at her mercy. She picks up a tent peg and a hammer. She lines it up over his temple and drives that stake in so hard it goes completely through his head and into the ground. Sisera is delivered into the hands of a woman!

As Barak approaches the tent, Jael goes out to meet him, saying, *"Come, and I will show you the man whom you are seeking"* (Judges 4:22). Jael turns over Sisera, the commander of Jabin's army, to Barak with a tent peg through his head!

Faith's Triumph is not delivered with impressive weapons. It was not horses or chariots or swords that delivered the sons of Israel. God does not need impressive weapons. He uses whatever is available; clay pitchers, torches, jawbones, a hammer and a tent peg, a few small fish and some loaves, a jar of oil and a little meal. It seems *less* is always *more* with God. And even wimps like Gideon and Barak enter the Master Architect's Faith Hall of Fame when they submit to God and use whatever means He inspires to live in enduring faith and deliver His people from the enemy's oppression.

Barak, a less than courageous man who is humble enough to allow victory to be delivered to him through the hands of two women, demonstrates *Faith's Triumph*. Deborah shares the marquee on exhibit #18 because she was willing to lead a seemingly defenseless army into war. Her enduring faith speaks on. Jael shares Barak's marquee because she used what she had, her tools for pitching the family's tents, to take out the commander of Israel's enemy. Her enduring faith speaks on. *Faith's Triumph* is delivered through humility and the willingness to use the resources God has placed at our disposal.

Chapter 15

FAITH'S PHYSICAL STRENGTH

Faith's Physical Strength

S amson demonstrates *Faith's Physical Strength* in exhibit #19. In the opening scene God speaks to the barren wife of Menoah during Israel's forty year servitude to the Philistines. He prophesies over her and gives her instructions, *"Then the angel of the LORD appeared to the woman and said to her, 'Behold now, you are barren and have borne no children, but you shall conceive and give birth to a son. Now therefore, be careful not to drink wine or strong drink, nor eat any unclean thing. For behold, you shall conceive and give birth to a son, and no razor shall come upon his head, for the boy shall be a Nazirite to God from the womb; and he shall begin to deliver Israel from the hands of the Philistines"* (Judges 13:3-5).

She runs to tell her husband. He is excited but he prays that God would come again and teach them what to do for the boy that is to be born. God obliges and comes to the woman once again. She runs to get Manoah. Manoah talks to God, *"Now when your words come to pass, what shall be the boy's mode of life and his vocation"* (Judges 13:12)? This is an important question. God answers, *"Let the woman pay attention to all that I said"* (Judges 13:13). In other words, "The woman knows."

In the next scene we find Samson grown up, hanging out in Timnah, Philistine territory. He has his eye on a woman there. Upon arriving home, he speaks to his father, *"I saw a woman in Timnah, one of the daughters of the Philistines; now therefore, get her for me as a wife."* Manoah objects. He thinks a woman from Israel would make a better wife, but Samson says, *"Get her for me, for she looks good to me"* (Judges 14:1-3). Samson does not seem to be thinking clearly here, but maybe God has something in mind for stirring things up with the Philistine oppressors.

Manoah obliges Samson's request and they head to Timnah. Samson is some distance ahead of his parents, when a young lion attacks Samson. It doesn't even faze him. He rips it apart with his bare hands and tosses it aside. His parents catch up to him now. As they walk on together he doesn't even mention the lion attack. In Timnah, Samson talks to the woman. She looks good to Samson and the arrangements are made before they return home.

Scene three is sometime later. Samson, his father, and his mother return to take his wife. He stops to look at the carcass of the lion he had killed. There is a swarm of bees and honey inside it. He scrapes the honey into his hands and eats it. Touching the carcass violates Nazirite law. He takes honey to his parents but he tells them nothing of the lion.

Scene four takes us to the wedding festivities. Samson uses his experience with the lion to devise a riddle for his Philistine guests. He promises them thirty linen wraps if they answer the riddle within seven days. If not, they owe him the same. They agree. He gives them the riddle, *"Out of the eater came something to eat, And out of the strong came something sweet"* (Judges 14:14). They are puzzled. The days are passing; one, two, three... They are getting desperate. They meet secretly with Samson's wife, threatening to burn her and her family if she doesn't tell them the answer. She is fearful! She begs Samson to tell her the answer to his riddle. Several days pass as she presses him. He gives in and tells her secrets he withheld from his parents.

It is now evening on the seventh day in scene five. The Philistine guests arrogantly answer Samson's riddle. He is angry. He shouts at them, *"If you had not plowed with my heifer, you would not have solved my riddle"* (Judges 14:18)! Samson storms off.

The next scene is in Ashkelon, a Philistine city some distance away. Samson kills thirty Philistine men and takes their clothes. This is an angry man. He is taking the clothes to the wedding guests, but he leaves in anger and goes home to his father's house.

Some time has passed and in scene seven Samson heads back to Timnah with a young goat for his wife. He speaks to his father-in-law, *"I will go in to my wife in her room"* (Judges 15:1). His father-in-law will not let him enter. He says, *"I really thought that you hated her intensely; so I gave her to your companion."* He has given Samson's wife to Samson's best man. The best man has consummated Samson's marriage. Samson is angry and says, *"This time I will be blameless in regard to the Philistines when I do them harm."* (Judges 15:2-3) Trouble brews.

Samson catches foxes, dozens of them with incredible speed and strength. He pairs them off by tying their tails together. He ties torches to the tails of each pair. He lights the torches and releases the foxes into the standing grain fields of the Philistines. There are hundreds of foxes. Everything burns up; the shocks, the standing wheat, the vineyards, and the olive yards.

Anger escalates when the Philistines find out the reason for the fires and go to the house of Samson's wife. They take his wife and her father and burn them to death. This woman received the very thing she deceptively tried to avoid. She would have been better off to trust Samson to protect her and her father with his supernatural strength. Self-protection never works, especially when devised through the means of deception.

In scene eight a very angry Samson speaks, *"Since you act like this, I will surely take revenge on you, but after that I will quit"* (Judges 15:7). There he goes, swinging. He is ruthless with them, taking out a multitude of Philistines before heading off to the mountains to hide out.

The Philistines gather an army and set up camp in Judah. They tell the men of Judah they want Samson. Three thousand men of Judah head out to find him. When they find Samson they speak, *"We have come to bind you so that we may give you into the hands of the Philistines."* Samson replies, *"Swear to me that you will not kill me"* (Judges 15:12). They agree and bind him with two new ropes and bring him out. The Philistines shout. They have their man. But he snapped those ropes like they were flax. Picking up a jawbone of a donkey, he swings it like a sword taking out man after Philistine man. Incredible!

Samson speaks; *"With the jawbone of a donkey, Heaps upon heaps, with the jawbone of a donkey I have killed a thousand men"* (Judges 15:16). He tosses the jawbone aside. 1000 Philistines killed with the jawbone of a donkey – God's one man army.

Samson looks famished. He calls out to God, *"You have given this great deliverance by the hand of Your servant, and now shall I die of thirst and fall into the hands of the uncircumcised"*(Judges 15:18)? Samson thinks it's all over. But water begins to gush from that hollow in the ground and Samson drinks, looking revived. What do we make of this man who seems to experience both trouble *and* the power of God? What is it that has given him entrance into Faith's Hall of Fame?

In scene nine we find an older Samson. He has been judging Israel for twenty years or so. He seems restless. On the move, he comes to Gaza where he spots a harlot. He goes into her house. Knowing Samson is in their city, the Gazites devise a plan. They'll wait the night by the closed gate of the city and kill him in the morning light. But Samson isn't going to wait until morning though. It is only midnight but here he comes. It looks like more trouble. As he nears the gate, Samson grabs the doors, lifting them *and* the posts right out of the ground. What incredible strength! He is carrying them away, right up the mountain. There will be no trouble tonight. This guy sleeps with a prostitute and immediately exhibits *faith's physical strength*. What are we to make of this? Will this exhibit explain?

Samson, in scene ten, is in the valley of Sorek. He is in love with another foreign woman named Delilah. This man of faith sure has a weakness for foreign women. This is his third Philistine woman and the previous two brought nothing but trouble. The Philistine lords talk to Delilah, each offering her 1100 pieces of silver to find the source of Samson's strength. Will this woman's love override her greed? She talks to Samson, *"Please tell me where your great strength is and how you may be bound to afflict you"* (Judges 16:6)? I guess not. I wonder if she could have been any more direct. This ought to send him on his way.

What is Samson *doing*? He gives her instructions on how he might be bound. He should be running. If he gives this woman any information she will only want more. Why do we think we can fool around on the riverbank without sliding in?

She does exactly what he told her, tying him up with seven fresh cords. She is hollering, *"The Philistines are upon you, Samson!"* This is a setup. But Samson is snapping those cords like bowstring in a fire. Surely he will ditch this woman now. Delilah cries, upset with Samson for deceiving her. She begs him to tell her the truth.

This Faith Hall of Famer cannot be stupid enough to continue engaging in this woman's chicanery. But he does. He is giving her further information. Does he think she will be satisfied with this? The same thing happens again. She ties him up as he instructed. The Philistines come out at her cue and he again snaps the ropes like thread. This should end their relationship.

She begs Samson for the truth. He answers her, *"If you will weave the seven locks of my hair with the web and fasten it with a pin, then I shall become weak and be like any other man"* (Judges 16:13). This is incredible! Can't he see that with each encounter she gets him to divulge information closer to the truth? Is this information in this exhibit for our benefit? Is it possible that we unknowingly behave in like manner? Can we be so blind to deception that we fool around with it until it becomes dangerous? What does Samson's exhibit demonstrate regarding enduring faith? Maybe he will now run from this woman's sophistry of love.

No, he does not. He is confidently asleep in her home. Once again she does as he instructed, pinning his hair to the loom. As dangerously close as this is to revealing his Nazirite vow and God's power as the source of his strength, he still pulls the pin of the loom free and overpowers the Philistines.

This has to be it. How can he trust this woman? But she continues, *"How can you say, 'I love you,' when your heart is not with me?"* She is putting the pressure on Samson. It looks like he is caving. Exasperated, he tells her about his Nazirite vow and how a razor has never touched his head, *"If I am shaved, then my strength will leave me and I shall become weak and be like any other man"* (Judges 16:17). She knows she has the truth this time.

Delilah sends messengers to the lords of the Philistines to tell them the news. They come, money in hand. She entices Samson to sleep in her lap. He *cannot* be so deceived not to see what is coming. Can he? Apparently he can. As he sleeps, a man comes into her room and shaves Samson's head.

Delilah shouts once again, *"The Philistines are upon you, Samson!"* He tries to shake himself free, but he cannot, for the power of God has departed from him. The Philistines gouge out his eyes. Must be a little insurance; if his strength does return, he'll be defenseless to their blows. They bind him with bronze chains. He cannot break them now.

In the final scene in exhibit #19, Samson is a grinder in prison and his hair has grown out once again. The Philistines have a party and celebrate their capture of Samson with sacrifices to their god Dagon. They give Dagon the credit rather than the deceptions of a greedy woman. This must, as men, make them feel safer. They call for Samson to amuse them. They bring Samson in, standing him between the pillars of the building. They laugh and mock him.

A boy holds Samson's hand. Samson speaks to him, *"Let me feel the pillars on which the house rests, that I may lean against them."*

The boy guides Samson's hands to the pillars. Samson calls out to the Lord, *"O Lord GOD, please remember me and please strengthen me just this time, O God, that I may at once be avenged of the Philistines for my two eyes"* (Judges 16:26-28). He grasps the pillars and shouts, *"Let me die with the Philistines!"* He pushes the pillars over. The building falls in, crushing those inside and killing the 3000 men and women on the roof.

Samson killed more Philistines at his death than he did in his life. Samson's concern was vengeance for his two eyes, but God's concern was the deliverance of His people Israel.

Samson gained membership into *Faith's Hall of Fame* and yet struggled to find the destiny of his calling. He ruled as judge over Israel for twenty years and yet fought to control the passions that raged within him. Why didn't the Master Architect choose to display any of Samson's activity as judge over Israel? Why has He displayed to us a faith man who loved women so deeply that it caused them to take advantage of him, deceiving and betraying him? Could it be that the Master Architect desires for us to "see" some unusual characteristics of faith?

From this exhibit we see that *faith's physical strength* was supernaturally supplied to get a man of faith out of trouble that he had gotten himself into. *That* concept is contrary to religious thinking! This places Paul's revelation of divine energy into another category. As enduring faith men and women might we use Colossians 1:29 *"For this purpose also I labor, striving according to His power, which mightily works within me."* to rid ourselves of trouble that we get ourselves into?

Is it possible that the Master Architect wants us to know that personal weakness does not exclude us from obtaining membership into Faith's Hall of Fame? From Samson's exhibit it is apparent there is no formula for membership. Samson endured, relying on God for his strength in spite of his mistakes and his struggle to find his destiny as Israel's deliverer. This fact is what placed Samson's name in the hall and his story in this exhibit. Here we have a man whose last act was to call on God for the strength to take his own life and die with the Philistines, yet he ends up demonstrating for us *faith's physical strength* in the Master Architect's Faith Hall of Fame. May we continue to endure by drawing on *faith's physical strength* in spite of our own missteps and our own struggle to find the destiny of our calling.

Chapter 16

FAITH'S BOLDNESS

Faith's Boldness

In exhibit #20 Jephthah demonstrates *Faith's Boldness*. The exhibit opens with the people of Gilead, many from the tribe of Gad who settled east of the Jordan, crying out to God for deliverance from the Ammonites. The leaders of the people speak to one another, *"Who is the man who will begin to fight against the sons of Ammon? He shall become head over all the inhabitants of Gilead"* (Judges 10:18).

This next scene takes us back in time to a young boy being harassed by other boys. "Jephthah, you're a bastard." They say ugly things about the boy's mother, even calling her a whore. Jephthah cries, the pain of rejection on his face.

The scene transforms. The boys are grown up now. The ones who were teasing Jephthah now holler at him and shove him saying, *"You shall not have an inheritance in our father's house, for you are the son of another woman"* (Judges 11:2). These boys are Jephthah's half-brothers. Since he is the son of a harlot their father went into, they want to cut him out of his share of the family inheritance. They drive him away. No bastard will have a share in their father's wealth.

In scene three we find Jephthah in the land of Tob. He appears to be the leader of some sort of gang. The ones who follow him appear to be wicked and worthless. But they are devoted to him. They listen to his commands. Jephthah must be the leader of the notorious Tob gang. It is rumored that the leader is a valiant warrior. They say he has taught the gang of rabble-rousers the art of war. Jephthah must have found a deviant way to rise above his child-hood rejection. This is a strange man to find in Faith's Hall of Fame.

The elders of Gilead come into Jephthah's camp. They talk to him, *"Come and be our chief that we may fight against the sons of Ammon."* Jephthah is angry. He speaks, *"Did you not hate me and drive me from my father's house? So why have you come to me now when you are in trouble?"* The elders respond, *"For this reason we have now returned to you, that you may go with us and fight with the sons of Ammon and become head over all the inhabitants of Gilead"* (Judges 11:6-8). This interests Jephthah and he goes with them.

Scene four takes us back to Gilead. The people declare Jephthah their leader and chief. He prepares messengers to send to the king of Ammon. His message is a very bold argument establishing Israel's right to possess the land they are on. His aim is to avoid war if possible.

As the messengers return, it is apparent the king of Ammon has disregarded Jephthah's message. His appeal has had no effect. No matter. The Spirit of the Lord comes upon Jephthah. He swiftly moves to make war against Ammon. He prays, *"If You will indeed give the sons of Ammon into my hand, then it shall be that whatever comes out of the doors of my house to meet me when I return in peace from the sons of Ammon, it shall be the LORD'S, and I will offer it up as a burnt offering"* (Judges 11:30-31). This is a rashly spoken vow. Hopefully he knows what he is doing. Nevertheless, he is now leading his army to war. They attack and achieve miraculous success. The hand of the Lord is surely in this. The sons of Israel subdue the sons of Ammon.

Scene five takes us to Jephthah's house. As Jephthah returns from his victory, his daughter comes out to meet him, singing and dancing with tambourines. Oh no! The vow! Jephthah tears his clothes. He speaks to her, *"Alas, my daughter! You have brought me very low, and you are among those who trouble me; for I have given my word to the LORD, and I cannot take it back."* He is deeply troubled, moaning about her being his only child, no other daughters or a son. She speaks, *"My father, you have given your word to the LORD; do to me as you have said, since the LORD has avenged you of your enemies, the sons of Ammon. Let this thing be done for me; let me alone two months, that I may go to the mountains and weep because of my virginity, I and my companions"* (Judges 11:35-37).

His daughter knows that her father cannot go back on his vow to the Lord. Since she obviously does not qualify for burnt offering, she will have to spend her life devoted to God by perpetual virginity. She will not be able to carry out her part in the life of Israel, keeping her family alive in this great nation. There will never be a child to carry on the name Jephthah. This man of faith appears to be a foolish vow maker. But the plaque on the exhibit states he judged Israel six years.

This man of enduring faith was born in less than exemplary cir-cumstances, negatively impacting his societal position. Jephthah suffered abuse at the hands of his own family and peers, even-tually being driven to pursue a life of crime. And yet this man of enduring faith had the boldness to rise up as the leader and judge over Israel. Even though he may have been a stupid vow maker, he is named as a member in Faith's Hall of Fame. *Faith's boldness* caused Jephthah to rise above his ignoble birth, his detrimental childhood, and his notorious vocation. *Faith's boldness* will allow us to overcome anything in our past and take us to a position we never dreamed possible.

Chapter 17

FAITH'S UTTER RELIANCE

Faith's Utter Reliance

E xhibit #21 reveals a lad named David who exemplifies *Faith's Utter Reliance*. This exhibit opens with the prophet Samuel standing before a tall, well-built young man. Jesse, the young man's father speaks, "Samuel, this is Eliab, my oldest son." God shows us what Samuel is thinking, *"Surely the Lord's anointed is standing before Him"* (1 Samuel 16:6). The Lord speaks, *"Do not look at his appearance or at the height of his stature, because I have rejected him; for God sees not as man sees, for man looks at the outward appearance, but the LORD looks at the heart"* (1 Samuel 16:7). Samuel searches for the next king of Israel. I wonder what God sees in Eliab's heart that Samuel has missed?

Samuel shakes his head. Jesse calls out, "Abinidab, come here." Abinidab walks over to Samuel. Samuel responds, *"Neither has the Lord chosen this one."* Jesse calls his next son, Shammah. No, it's not him either. Five more of Jesse's sons pass before Samuel. Samuel responds, *"The Lord has not chosen these."* He says to Jesse, *"Are these all the children?"* Jesse replies, *"There* remains yet the youngest, and behold, he is tending the sheep." Samuel tells Jesse, *"Send and bring him; for we will not sit down until he comes here"* (1 Samuel 16:8-11).

Jesse's youngest son enters. He is a mere teenager, but handsome in appearance. The Lord speaks, *"Arise, anoint him, for he is the one"* (1 Samuel 16:12). Samuel pours the horn of oil he brought onto this lad's head. His brothers watch with looks of wonder on their faces. Samuel departs.

In scene two we find King Saul and his army camped on the mountain on one side of the valley of Elah. The Philistine army is on the mountainside across the valley. A very large warrior comes down from the Philistine camp into the valley. He's got to be twelve or thirteen feet tall! He wears full body armor. On a man that size it has to weigh 300 pounds. His spear looks like a beam. He faces the ranks of the Israeli army shouting, *"Why do you come out to draw up in battle array? Am I not the Philistine and you servants of Saul? Choose a man for yourselves and let him come down to me. If he is able to fight with me and kill me, then we will become your servants; but if I prevail against him and kill him, then you shall become our servants and serve us. I defy the ranks of Israel this day; give me a man that we may fight together"* (1 Samuel 17:8-10).

Fear sweeps across the Israeli ranks. One of the soldiers speaks to another, "Eliab, What are we going to do? This giant, Goliath, has been taunting us twice a day for forty days now. We've got no soldier who can take this guy! Maybe we should devise some other plan." The soldier responds, "Leave it Shammah. You and Abinadab just stay out of the way. Our father isn't looking for heroics from us." These are the three oldest sons of Jesse, the brothers of the lad who was anointed.

In scene three Jesse talks to David, his youngest son, the lad who was anointed. *"Take now for your brothers an ephah of this roasted grain and these ten loaves and run to the camp to your brothers. Bring also these ten cuts of cheese to the commander of their thousand, and look into the welfare of your brothers, and bring back news of them. For Saul and they and all the men of Israel are in the valley of Elah, fighting with the Philistines"*(1 Samuel 17:17-19). David leaves with the supplies.

We are once again at the battleground in scene four. David arrives with the supplies. He just dropped off the supplies with the baggage keeper and runs to the front lines. This kid is nuts! He greets his brothers just as that giant Goliath comes. He shouts the same taunts. David listens. The army turns and runs away in fear. David listens to some of the soldiers talking, *"Have you seen this man who is coming up? Surely he is coming up to defy Israel. And it will be that the king will enrich the man who kills him with great riches and will give him his daughter and make his father's house free in Israel"* (1 Samuel 17:25).

David is fired up and replies to them, *"What will be done for the man who kills this Philistine and takes away the reproach from Israel? For who is this uncircumcised Philistine, that he should taunt the armies of the living God"* (1 Samuel 17:26)? The soldiers tell him that Saul will certainly reward the one who kills Goliath just as they had spoken.

Eliab, his oldest brother has been listening to this exchange. He is visibly angry and speaks, *"Why have you come down? And with whom have you left those few sheep in the wilderness? I know your insolence and the wickedness of your heart; for you have come down in order to see the battle"* (1 Samuel 17: 28).

Ouch! Hearing his youngest brother question why someone hasn't accepted Goliath's challenge pricked his heart. This must be what God saw that Samuel could not. David's older brother's pride has just been pricked. He is jealous of his little brother and accuses him of things that are in his own heart. This is telling; oftentimes the things we are most critical of in others are the very things we harbor in our own hearts.

David looks astonished. He replies to Eliab, *"What have I done now? Was it not just a question"* (1Samuel 17:29)? David walks away. He inquires the same of others. He wants to fully understand what the problem is. They answer him as before.

In scene five we find Saul sending for David. Apparently someone has told Saul about this brave speaking lad. David enters and speaks to Saul, *"Let no man's heart fail on account of him; your servant will go and fight with this Philistine"* (1 Samuel 17:32). These are brave words for a kid who is not even of age to serve in the army.

Saul doesn't know whether to be astonished or to laugh. He responds, *"You are not able to go against this Philistine to fight with him; for you are but a youth while he has been a warrior from his youth"* (1 Samuel 17:33).

Look at the fire in David's eyes. He is unflinching and replies, *"Your servant was tending his father's sheep. When a lion or a bear came and took a lamb from the flock, I went out after him and attacked him, and rescued it from his mouth; and when he rose up against me, I seized him by his beard and struck him and killed him. Your servant has killed both the lion and the bear; and this uncir- cumcised Philistine will be like one of them, since he has taunted the armies of the living God. The LORD who delivered me from*

141

the paw of the lion and from the paw of the bear, He will deliver me from the hand of this Philistine" (1 Samuel 17:34-37). David gives Saul three reasons why he is qualified to take on Goliath. With his hands he killed a lion and a bear and with his heart he has faith in God.

Saul hasn't seen anything like this before. He seems to be at a loss for words. He speaks to David, *"Go, and may the LORD be with you"* (1 Samuel 17:37). It is obvious that Saul does not believe this lad is God's method for delivering Israel from this giant. Nevertheless, the king gives David his uniform. Saul places his helmet on David's head and straps his armor on David's body. David, taking Saul's sword, tries to walk. It is hulking and clumsy. David speaks, *"I cannot go with these, for I have not tested them"* (1 Samuel 17:39). He takes off all of Saul's garments and armor. This young man of enduring faith displays *utter reliance* on God alone! He picks up his shepherd's staff and leaves.

Scene six finds David at the brook in the valley. He reaches down. He must be thirsty. No, he looks at stones from the brook. He throws one in his shepherd's bag. He looks at more stones. He throws another in the bag. One more goes in. And now two more stones go in for a total of five. These must be for the sling he has draped over his shoulder. The giant approaches David. His shield bearer is in front of him. This is a daunting scene. Goliath's shield is bigger than David. Goliath laughs and speaks to David, *"Am I a dog, that you come to me with sticks? Come to me, and I will give your flesh to the birds of the sky and the beasts of the field"* (1 Samuel 17:43-44).

David is unfazed. He replies, *"You come to me with a sword, a spear, and a javelin, but I come to you in the name of the LORD of hosts, the God of the armies of Israel, whom you have taunted. This day the LORD will deliver you up into my hands, and I will strike you down and remove your head from you. And I will give the dead bodies of the army of the Philistines this day to the birds of the sky and the wild beasts of the earth, that all the earth may know that there is a God in Israel, and that all this assembly may know that the LORD does not deliver by sword or by spear; for the battle is the LORD'S and He will give you into our hands"* (1 Samuel 17:45-47). These are the incredibly confident words of *faith's utter reliance.* David is not comparing Goliath's size, armor, or ability with his own. He is comparing Goliath with God and Goliath comes up very far short!

Goliath is riled up! He advances toward David leaving his shield bearer behind. His sword is still sheathed. He intends to rip David apart with his bare hands. David, unafraid, runs toward the giant, reaching in his bag. He places a stone in his sling. He now whips the sling into motion. As Goliath thunders toward David, David releases the stone. The stone hits the giant right in his forehead! He stumbles, falling face down on the ground! David took this giant down without any weapons but a sling! Standing over Goliath, David draws Goliath's sword from its sheath. David cuts off Goliath's head with his own sword, just like he said he would do!

The Philistine army flees. Either they are afraid of this unlikely giant killer, or they are unwilling to fulfill their part of Goliath's agreement to serve Israel. Maybe it is both. Nevertheless, the Israeli army is shouting and chasing the Philistines. They are taking them out by the multitudes and plundering their camps. This is an incredible turn of events for the Israelites. It is amazing what *faith's utter reliance* can accomplish.

David puts Goliath's weapons in his tent. David, who has Goliath's head in his hand, goes to the king with Abner, the commander of Saul's army. Saul speaks to him, *"Whose son are you young man?"* David replies, *"I am the son of your servant Jesse the Bethlehemite"* (1 Samuel 17:58). This kid just took out the biggest threat to Israel's freedom and he tells Saul, *"I am the son of your servant."*

Faith's utter reliance remains humble in the midst of astounding victory. *Faith's utter reliance* never looks at one's own ability or inability. *Faith's utter reliance* only considers the ability of God. *Faith's utter reliance* does not depend on the protection from another man, even if it is from someone as noble and powerful as a king. *Faith's utter reliance* uses what God has given to defend and protect his people even if it is as simple as a sling and a stone!

Chapter 18

FAITH'S INTEGRITY

Faith's Integrity

In exhibit #22 we find the Prophet Samuel demonstrating *Faith's Integrity*. In the opening scene he is a mere boy ministering to the Lord before Eli the priest in the house of the Lord. The boy Samuel lies in his bed in the temple. *"Samuel,"* a voice cries out. Samuel gets up and goes to Eli. *"Here I am,"* he says. Eli responds, *"I did not call, lie down again."* Samuel returns to bed. *"Samuel,"* the voice speaks again. He runs to Eli again, *"Here I am, for you called me."* Eli tells him to go lie down again. It happens again and Samuel runs to Eli. Eli gets up. He contemplates something and speaks, *"Go lie down, and it shall be if He calls you, that you shall say, 'Speak, Lord, for thy servant is listening.'"* Samuel returns to lie down.

Look at that. It is the Lord, standing before Samuel and calling out with the same voice as before, *"Samuel! Samuel!"* Samuel sits up answering, *"Speak, for Thy servant is listening."* The Lord responds, *"Behold, I am about to do a thing in Israel at which both ears of everyone who hears it will tingle. In that day I will carry out*

*against Eli all that I have spoken concerning his house, from begin-
ning to end. For I have told him that I am about to judge his house
forever for the iniquity which he knew, because his sons brought a
curse on themselves and he did not rebuke them. Therefore I have
sworn to the house of Eli that the iniquity of Eli's house shall not
be atoned for by sacrifice or offering forever"* (1 Samuel 3:11-14).

The next morning, in scene two, Samuel opens the doors of
the temple. He avoids Eli, afraid to tell Eli of the vision. Surely he
does not want to distress the old priest he reveres as a father and
spiritual guide. He is not required to. God did not tell him to deliver
this message to Eli, but he knows that Eli will probably ask. Eli
calls, *"Samuel, my son."* Samuel cringes but responds, *"Here I am."*

"What is the word that He spoke to you?" Eli asks, *"Please do
not hide it from me. May God do so to you, and more also, if you
hide anything from me of all the words that He spoke to you"* (1
Samuel 3:16-17). That puts the pressure on the boy. He speaks,
telling Eli every word that God spoke to him. He hides nothing. As
a boy, Samuel demonstrates *faith's integrity*.

In scene three of the exhibit we find the Prophet Samuel, as
a man, speaking to Israel, *"If you return to the LORD with all your
heart, remove the foreign gods and the Ashtaroth from among you
and direct your hearts to the LORD and serve Him alone; and He
will deliver you from the hand of the Philistines"* (1Samuel 7:3). The
people respond to this man of integrity. All of Israel recognizes that
Samuel has replaced Eli as a spokesman for God. They remove
the Baals and the Ashtaroth, the gods of the Canaanites. They talk
about serving the Lord alone. Samuel instructs Israel to gather in
Mizpah. They obey. They draw water and pour it out before the

Lord as a symbol of pouring out their hearts to God. They declare a fast for the day. These people are repentant.

Scene four takes us to the camp of the Philistine army. They have heard of Israel's illegal national gathering at Mizpah. They regard this as a breach of treaty with this servant nation and mobilize their army against Israel. The sons of Israel, having been stripped of their arms by their Philistine overseers, are afraid. They cry out to Samuel, *"Do not cease to cry out to the Lord our God for us, that He may save us from the hand of the Philistines"* (1 Samuel 7:8). Samuel offers a suckling lamb to God as a burnt offering. He cries out to the Lord. God answers this man who demonstrates faith's integrity.

The Philistines draw near in battle! What is *that*? I've never heard thunder like that before! It is incredibly loud and focused right over the Philistine army. They are confused. They cannot handle the noise. They are stumbling over each other as they try to run and escape the thunder. The men of Israel pursue and overtake the Philistine army. They retake city after city that the Philistines have taken from Israel. Samuel takes a stone and sets it as a memorial between Mizpah and Shen. He calls it Ebenezer, crying out, *"Thus far the Lord has helped us"* (1 Samuel 7:12). Israel is delivered from the hands of the Philistines by a miracle wrought by the man exemplifying *faith's integrity*.

In scene five we find Samuel as an old man appointing his sons Joel and Abijah judges over Israel. But his sons do not walk in the integrity their father modeled. They use their authority for personal gain. They accept bribes, stoop to extortion, and pervert the justice their office is designed to provide for Israel. Samuel's sons have become just like Eli's, whose judgment God revealed to Samuel.

The elders of Israel gather together. Coming to Samuel they address him, *"Behold, you have grown old, and your sons do not walk in your ways. Now appoint a king for us to judge us like all the nations"* (1 Samuel 8:5). The people of Israel do not want Samuel's corrupt sons ruling over them when he dies, so they ask him to give them a king to rule over them. Samuel is not pleased. He feels they are rejecting him. As Samuel prays, the Lord tells him the people are not rejecting him but rather they are rejecting the Lord from being king over them. God tells him to go ahead and give them a king but to warn them what a king will extract from them and their children.

Samuel tells the people all the negative aspects of living under the rule of a king. They refuse to listen to him. *"No, but there shall be a king over us, that we also may be like all the nations, that our king may judge us and go out before us and fight our battles"* (1 Samuel 8:19-20). The Lord tells Samuel to give the people what they want. That is *so* God! He never overrides the will of his creation. Freewill is freewill. So enduring faith's man of integrity now establishes the kingdom of Israel.

In the next scene all of Israel has gathered at Gilgal. Samuel pronounces Saul as king over Israel. Samuel appears to be disappointed as he speaks to the people, *"Behold, I have listened to your voice in all that you said to me and I have appointed a king over you. Now, here is the king walking before you, but I am old and gray, and behold my sons are with you. And I have walked before you from my youth even to this day. Here I am; bear witness against me before the LORD and His anointed. Whose ox have I taken, or whose donkey have I taken, or whom have I defrauded? Whom have I oppressed, or from whose hand have I taken a bribe to blind my eyes with it? I will restore it to you"* (1 Samuel 12:1-3).

Samuel defends his administration as he relinquishes leadership over Israel to Saul. He asks the people if he has ever dealt with them in any way other than in honesty and integrity. They answer, *"You have not defrauded us or oppressed us or taken anything from any man's hand"* (1 Samuel 12:4).

Samuel describes the history of God's preservation of the nation of Israel and His righteous acts toward them. After all this, he says, *"You said to me, 'No, but a king shall reign over us,' although the Lord your God was your king. Now therefore, here is the king whom you have chosen, whom you have asked for, and behold, the Lord has set a king over you"* (1 Samuel 12:12-13). He warns the people and their king to obey the Lord. He is still displeased and wants the people to know they have sinned against God by rejecting God and requesting a king. He tells them to watch right now and see, *"Is it not the wheat harvest today? I will call to the LORD, that He may send thunder and rain. Then you will know and see that your wickedness is great which you have done in the sight of the LORD by asking for yourselves a king"* (1 Samuel 12:17). Thunder and rain in the middle of wheat harvest? Highly unlikely! That would definitely be a sign for these folks that God is not pleased with their decision.

Samuel calls to the Lord. Thunder explodes from the sky. It rains torrentially. The people are in fear of the Lord and Samuel. They call out to Samuel, *"Pray for your servants to the LORD your God, so that we may not die, for we have added to all our sins this evil by asking for ourselves a king."* Samuel responds, *"Do not fear. You have committed all this evil, yet do not turn aside from following the LORD, but serve the LORD with all your heart. You must not turn aside, for then you would go after futile things which can not profit or deliver, because they are futile. For the LORD will not abandon His people on account of His great name, because the LORD has been pleased to make you a people for Himself. Moreover, as for me, far be it from me that I should sin against the LORD by ceasing to pray for you; but I will instruct you in the good and right way"* (1 Samuel 12:19-23).

Samuel makes it clear the people had sinned but that it was now over and forgiven. He instructs them to proceed with establishing their kingdom under Saul and make the best of it by serving the Lord and Him alone. Samuel, demonstrating *faith's integrity*, takes his role seriously and commits to pray for and instruct this people in spite of their rejection of his prophetic office for the office of a king. *Faith's integrity* refuses to reject a people even when the people reject the man manifesting *faith's integrity*.

Samuel is a man who exhibits *faith's integrity* by being a truthful, just, godly leader as a boy, as a man, as a prophet, and as a rejected spokesman for God's best interests of His people. Faith's *ultimate* integrity is manifested in praying for and instructing people who have chosen someone else to listen to and someone else to lead them. We can manifest faith's integrity by refusing to reject those who reject our advice, our ministry, or us. We exhibit *faith's integrity* when we continue to love and instruct those whose lives are a mess because they refused to listen.

Chapter 19

FAITH'S CONSUMMATION

Faith's Consummation

In exhibit #23, the last exhibit in Faith's Hall of Fame, we find those whom the Master Architect calls "others" manifesting "Faith's Consummation" for us. This is not a pleasant exhibit. One of the "others" is tortured. Offered the option of "shrinking back" to walk by sight and be released, he says, "No! Enduring faith gains approval!" His torturer threatens to kill him in response. This enduring faith man tells his torturer, "I will obtain a better resurrection than any you might offer!"

Some of the "others" are in chains. Their captors whip them, laugh and mock them, call them stupid, rodents, and animals. They toss some into prison cells. In a ravine "others" are being stoned. Most are silent. Some cry out, "Enduring faith gains approval!" Look at that rig over there. Their captors are laying some of the "others" on that rack and sawing them in two. Some are put to death with the sword. What is *faith's consummation*? What does this last exhibit reveal to us about enduring faith?

In the next scene of the exhibit, "others" wander in deserts and mountains. They live in caves and holes in the ground. Their clothing is sheepskins and goatskins. Apparently they have chosen this life. And even though they do not conquer kingdoms, perform acts of righteousness, or close the mouths of lions, the Master Architect displays their lives as examples of men and women who gain approval through their faith. It must not be so much *what* we do, but *why* we do *what* we do that gains approval. The enduring faith of these "others" caused them to choose destitution, affliction, ill-treatment, and death. Death! *Faith's consummation* is the death of our earthly tenure. Regardless of what we choose to do, if we choose to do what we do on the basis of enduring faith, the culmination of an enduring walk of faith is the successful escape from our physical body with approval as the payoff.

Faith's consummation can only be realized through enduring faith. It is not something to be feared. It is something to be revered. The sign at the end of this exhibit states, *"But My righteous one shall live by faith; and if he shrinks back, My soul has no pleasure in him"* (Hebrews 11:38). The Master Architect does not want us to shrink back from *faith's consummation.* He wants us to view it as the culmination of enduring faith and the gateway to the city, which has foundations, whose architect and builder is God. So revere *faith's consummation* as you journey through life in enduring faith.

The Master Architect's Epilogue

The Master Architect's commentary on His display in this hall is written for us to peruse. It reads, "All of these faith heroes, regardless of their feats and their foibles, gained approval through their faith. Yet none of them received what was promised. My desire was to provide something better for everyone, including you. So, apart from you, I did not make them perfect. And that is what they desired. That is the promise that propelled them into a life of enduring faith. Every one of the heroes in My Faith's Hall of Fame looked to the future and believed in what I would do for them when I brought perfection into their world, when I came and lived as one of them. I have now brought perfection into the world in which they lived, and I invite you to emulate their enduring faith, look into history, and by faith receive the "something better" I have provided for all of you, perfection! In this hall you have so great a cloud of witnesses surrounding you, so lay aside every *encumbrance* and run with endurance the enduring faith race that I've set before you!" At the bottom it is signed, "The Master Architect". Below that is inscribed "Hebrews 11:39-12:1"

Here in the Master Architect's epilogue we have finally discovered our ninth and last *"ence"*–encumbrance. Do you remember our summation of Enduring Faith Gains Approval?

> Your confid*ence* pushes you to endur*ance*, giving you the assur*ance* that your rever*ence* to His Word will give you an inherit*ance* that will flow to your descend*ants*, which you view from a dist*ance*, in spite of your experi*ence*! So lay aside every encumbr*ance* to your confid*ence*!

Since the Master Architect's epilogue was derived from the beginning of His work in Hebrews 12, let's conclude our tour and explore the work to see if we can find more information about laying aside every encumbrance.

The curator of the hall is coming. He says we are not finished. There is one more exhibit. This one is a *must see*, displaying the consummation of the Master Architect's faith. He says it will provide information and inspiration for laying aside the encumbrances to our confidence. Let's follow him.

The Consummation of the Master Architect's Faith

This exhibit appears similar to the last one, yet there is an aura of joy in the air. Soldiers beat a man and strip him. They whip him and spit on him. They press a crown of thorns on his head. This is the Christ! This exhibit manifests for us the consummation of God's faith!

The Master Architect displays for us in the body of Jesus, His own physical death, the culmination of His journey of enduring faith. The soldiers demand that Jesus carry his own cross. His bloody and beaten body buckles under the weight of it. Through the streets of the city he drags His cross. He approaches a hill just outside the city walls. He can no longer stand underneath the weight. Soldiers commandeer another man to finish the trek to the site of the crucifixion.

The soldiers nail Jesus' hands and feet to His cross. They now place Him in an upright position. It is obvious He is in great pain and agony, and yet joy exudes from His eyes. It is the joy of the Master Architect's faith's consummation! Jesus knows this is the gateway for mankind's entrance into His city. He knows He is providing perfection for all of His creation who will receive it. It is for this joy He endures this cross. The shame they hurl at Jesus does not bother Him. You can see victory through the pain on His face as He dies the agonizing death of crucifixion.

In scene two of this exhibit, Jesus is seated at the right hand of the throne of God. His enduring faith brought the resurrection power of God onto the scene and burned life back into the body of the Christ. This resurrected Christ ascended into heaven and with Him were raised all the enduring faith men and women who were made alive in Him.

Give consideration to this. The Master Architect had that in mind for this exhibit. The sign on this display reads, "If you are weary, ready to lose heart; if you are encumbered by the sin which so easily entangles, consider this exhibit. If walking in enduring faith has tired you, consider Jesus who endured such hostility by sinners against Himself. Have you yet resisted to the point of shedding your blood? If you are reading this, you have not!" The Master Architect informs us that *consideration*, consideration of the endurance of the Christ, provides the *inspiration* to lay aside every *encumbrance* to our confidence.

The Master Architect displays the consummation of His faith to inspire us to remain steadfast. If we fix our eyes on *His* enduring faith we will not grow weary and lose heart (Heb. 12:3).

Jesus is the fountainhead of the long list of faith heroes displayed in this hall of faith. He is the originator of their faith, and like a locomotive, pulled this long train of faith heroes to their destination of approval through enduring faith. Every one of these faith heroes knew He created them. Every one of them knew that only He was their Savior. All of them gazed across the mountaintops of prophecy and placed their faith in Him while they waited for His arrival and the consummation of His faith.

The Master Architect desires that we too consider the conduct and courage that our Savior demonstrated while under fire. He knows if we will just hook up, like the faith heroes of old, we will be pulled to enduring faith's destination, *God's approval*!

Chapter 20

THE DISCIPLINE OF ENDURING FAITH

The Master Architect and the Discipline of Enduring Faith

This is an incredible hall of fame! Faith's Hall of Fame. As we exit this hall one final sign remains over the doors. It reads:

"It is for discipline that you *endure*. I deal with you as My children. When you participate in the discipline of *endurance*, it legitimizes your role as princes and princesses in My kingdom. I invite you to subject yourselves to the discipline of endurance by subjecting yourself to Me, the Father of spirits. If you do so, you will live."–The Master Architect (Hebrews 12:7-9)

The Master Architect is a Father to His children. He is a better parent than man, not worse. He does not demand something we are incapable of, that is, our holiness. But rather He shares with us His holiness. The *discipline of enduring faith*, fixing our eyes on Jesus, (Heb. 12:2) allows us to continually experience the benefits of *His* holiness. Hebrews 12:10 states, *"…but He disciplines us for our good, that we may share His holiness."*

The Master Architect's discipline is actually His *grace* extended toward us. His grace disciplines us and teaches us to live sensibly.

Titus 2:11-12 informs us, *"For the grace of God has appeared, bringing salvation to all men, instructing us to deny ungodliness and worldly desires and to live sensibly, righteously and godly in the present age."*

What a Father! His grace, his "not counting our sins against us", actually disciplines us to live sensibly. It is inside of the Master Architect's *grace* that we see the *discipline of enduring faith* keeping us subject to our Father. The Master Architect wants us to understand that His grace is not only sufficient, but actually superior to the erroneous concept that He would use accidents or sickness to discipline us. He would have us know that as we willingly subject ourselves to the Master Architect, (Heb. 12:9) He sends the Holy Spirit to discipline or *disciple* us as we live and abide in Christ, allowing the Holy Spirit to lead us, teach us, and show us the will of the Master Architect. True discipline is allowing the Holy Spirit to teach us the will of the Master Architect through His Word.

Hebrews 12:7 tells us, *"It is for discipline that you endure."* The Master Architect emphasizes that *it is for discipline that we endure, not that we are disciplined for the purpose of endurance.* We are to live a life of enduring faith. Living a life of enduring faith produces a life of discipline in us. The very theme of Faith's Hall of Fame is *endurance.* The Master Architect spoke of it directly in Hebrews 10:23, 32, 36, 38; 11:25, 27; 12:1-3, 7. It is clear that the discipline of which the Master Architect speaks is a discipline we subject ourselves to, that is, the discipline of enduring faith.

Hebrews 12:8 confirms it is the Master Architect's words, not accidents or sickness that disciplines us toward enduring faith. We are told, *"But if you are without discipline, of which all have become partakers, then you are illegitimate children and not sons."*

158

According to this verse all of His *legitimate* children are partakers of His discipline. They have subjected themselves to the Master Architect's words. They exercise the discipline of enduring faith. They fix their eyes on Jesus (Heb. 12:2).

Illegitimate children, those not in Christ, are excluded from this discipline. Since *all* of mankind is subject to accidents and sickness, the Master Architect *must be* referring to something else as discipline. Otherwise, would not sickness and accidents then be used as an agent for illegitimate children to claim legitimacy? Furthermore, if Jesus bore our sins, why would the Master Architect use sin to discipline us? He wouldn't. And if Jesus bore our sicknesses, why would the Master Architect use sickness to discipline us? He wouldn't. He would never use those things placed on His Son for our deliverance to prove we are His. In fact, Jesus Himself tells us in John 6:63, *"...the flesh profits nothing."* Nothing! There would be no profit in the Master Architect attempting to use physical means to discipline His children. God is spirit! This is why Jesus went on to say, *"It is the Spirit who gives life,"* and then tells us, *"...the words that I have spoken to you are spirit and are life"* (John 4:24).

The Master Architect's discipline is His Word instructing us in His ways. Instruction in His ways is what leads us in the discipline of enduring faith, and enduring faith is what gains approval (Heb. 11:2, 39). When we operate outside of the parameters of His ways we sow into rebellion. The Master Architect has told us that we will reap what we sow. Reaping what we sow is one of God's established spiritual laws. Some want to call what we reap God's discipline but what we reap is essentially what *we* deal into our own hand.

In the end it is not discipline the Master Architect is looking for, but what the *discipline of the Word* produces, that is, enduring faith. Jesus Himself revealed this truth when He asked this question in Luke 18:8 (AMP), *"However, when the Son of Man comes, will He find persistent faith on the earth?"* Remember, "It is good to have an end to journey toward, but it is the journey that matters in the end." (Ursula K. Le Guin)

Enduring faith gains approval! God the Father, the Master Architect, stated over and over again, *"The just shall live by faith"* (Habakkuk 2:4, Romans 1:17, Galatians 3:11, Hebrews 10:38). The Master Architect's invitation still remains; "I invite you to subject yourselves to the discipline of endurance by subjecting yourself to Me, the Father of spirits. If you do so, you will live!"

THE SUMMATION OF
ENDURING FAITH GAINS APPROVAL
Hebrews 10:32-12:11

Your **confid_ence_** pushes you to **endur_ance_**, giving you the **assur_ance_** that your **rever_ence_** to His Word will give you an **inherit_ance_** that will flow to your **descend_ants_**, which you view from a **dist_ance_**, in spite of your **experi_ence_**! So lay aside every **encumbr_ance_** to your **confid_ence_**!

ABOUT THE AUTHOR

Jerry is a husband, father, grandfather, and pastor who is on a journey to walk hand in hand with Jesus every day. While learning to live life at the pace of a walk, his greatest desire is to do so in humility, faith, grace and victory while encouraging other believers to join him on this journey.

Enduring Faith Gains Approval

is the 3rd book in Jerry Grieser's Trilogy of Faith series

Trilogy of Faith series

Harvesting God's Word

Discovering God's Original and Intentional System of Sowing and Reaping

Intelligent Faith

The Journey from Discovery to Destination

Enduring Faith Gains Approval

Focusing on Faith Instead of the Manifestation

Other Books by Jerry Grieser

God's House of Mirrors

Seeing Yourself from God's Perspective

Brokenness & The Strong Man's Gospel

Parallel Tracks to Access God's Power

CPSIA information can be obtained
at www.ICGtesting.com
Printed in the USA
FFHW012111161118
49420975-53762FF